DEATH
OF A
BARONET

ANTHONY HARRIS

DEATH OF A BARONET

THE LAWFORD HALL MURDER

BREWIN BOOKS

First published by
Brewin Books Ltd, 56 Alcester Road,
Studley, Warwickshire B80 7LG in 2011

www.brewinbooks.com

ISBN: 978-1-85858-472-0

A Cataloguing in Publication Record
for this title is available from the British Library.

Typeset in Sabon
Printed in Great Britain by
Hobbs the Printers Ltd.

Contents

Acknowledgements

I WOULD like to record my debt to the many individuals and members of staff at the following institutions, all of whom have been unfailingly helpful to me in pursuing my researches: the British Library; the Bodleian Library, Oxford; the Local Studies departments of Warwickshire Information and Library Services in Warwick and Rugby, especially Susan Gray; Coventry City Library; the Picture Library of the National Portrait Gallery; the National Archives, Kew; the Libraries, Archives and Guildhall Art Gallery section of the London Metropolitan Archives; the Sir John Soane's Museum; Dr Ruth Paley; Anne and John Grove, formerly of the Prince Hall Hotel, Devon; and, most of all, my wife, for bearing with patience and good humour the ridiculously long drawn-out birth pangs of this book.

The author and publisher also gratefully acknowledge permission to reproduce the following images:

> Plates 3 and 4: National Portrait Gallery, London; Plates 7 and 8: City of London, London Metropolitan Archives; Plate 13: Warwickshire County Record Office (item ret: DR 176/4); Plates 14-17 are reproduced by kind permission of Warwickshire County Council, Library and Information Service.

Prologue

Saturday 9th September 1780
St Botolph's churchyard, Newbold-on-Avon, Warwickshire

THE BODY, still in its grave-clothes, is lifted out of the lead-lined coffin and reverently laid on the slabbed tomb. The sightless eyes stare out from a face unnaturally swollen. The lips are retracted to reveal teeth and gums as black as the face and throat. Sir Theodosius Boughton, seventh Baronet, of Lawford Parva in the county of Warwickshire, only four days earlier laid to rest in the family crypt, lies exposed to the bright September sun.

At this time exhumation is not a discreetly screened, middle of the night affair, but conducted in the full light of day for all to witness, and the throng of estate workers, tenants, villagers and sensation-seekers from the surrounding towns – some five hundred in all, filling every nook and cranny of the churchyard – edges closer. The gossip and rumour that has swept the county in the eleven days since the death of the young man – still a year short of attaining his majority – has reached its climax.

There have already been two efforts at an autopsy, when the body was still at Lawford Hall. But before the first attempt it had lain uncoffined for four days, the weather had been exceptionally warm and putrefaction had already reached an advanced stage. The three medical men present – Dr Rattray and Mr Wilmer from Coventry and Mr Thomas Powell, the Rugby apothecary who had attended the baronet in his final illness, treating it was said a long-standing syphilitic complaint and concocting the potion that had preceded the fatal convulsions – hastily agreed among themselves that any investigation would serve no useful purpose and the body was prepared for burial. However, Mr Samuel Bucknill, surgeon of Rugby and, in his own estimation at least, a coming man is made of sterner stuff. He has, or so he claims, sat at the feet of the great Mr John Hunter, the leading surgeon-anatomist of the day – and whose path he will cross once again before this affair reaches its dramatic conclusion.

Seizing this chance to enhance his reputation at the expense of his more squeamish colleagues – mere 'country practitioners', as he loftily terms them – he immediately contacted Sir William Wheler, the young man's guardian, and offered to perform the task. Sir William consented, on condition that his personal physician, Mr Snow from Southam, was also present. However, the latter did not arrive at the Hall until several hours after the agreed time, by when Bucknill had left, in considerable dudgeon, with the body still unopened.

And so, once again, the coffin lid was sealed, with John Crooke, the estate's plumber, complaining that the frequent soldering was making the lead too hot to touch. At seven o'clock that same evening the funeral service was at last held and the body committed to the crypt.

This though has only served to increase the talk of foul play and yet another autopsy has been ordered to establish once and for all the cause of death. It has been arranged for the following Saturday, which is particularly fortunate for the group of boys from Rugby School who have clearly decided that an exhumation, and of a seventh baronet no less, beats Latin prep as a pastime hands down.

Among them is fourteen year-old Henry Halford, whose experience this day will set him on a path that is to lead to the position of physician to the unfortunate King George III and three other monarchs and the presidency of the Royal College of Physicians.

Although all the medical men involved, including Mr Snow, are present, Mr Bucknill has again offered to conduct the investigation. However, the late summer heatwave has continued, the coffin has by now been soldered and unsoldered six times, and as the body is laid on the tomb the stench of decay is even more overpowering.

Forewarned, Mr Bucknill has a cloth dipped in vinegar tied round his mouth and nostrils and wears, also soaked in vinegar, a waggoner's smock – fittingly rural substitutes for his surgeon's mask and gown. The mob falls silent as, instruments in hand, he steps forward but then, without warning, he lurches back, pushes his way through the astonished crowd and disappears from view.

The remaining doctors, the coroner, the jury members already sworn for the inquest that is to follow, exchange glances and whisper uncertainly among themselves. For one of the jurymen, Robert Oneley, the event has already taken on a special significance for it is on his family's tomb that the coffin rests – a tomb in which he himself will lie some ten years hence.

They turn to the small group of family members, standing a little way off. In particular, they look for guidance to Lady Anna Maria Boughton, who has steeled herself to witness this final desecration of her only son, but she remains stony-faced and silent.

The onlookers, fearing that they are to be deprived of their day's entertainment, are growing increasingly restive but then, after half an hour, Mr Bucknill returns. He offers no explanation for his conduct but has in fact retreated to a nearby house and only after imbibing several glasses of wine does he feel sufficiently fortified to continue with his self-appointed task.

His comrades, for all of whom this is a first exhumation, reluctantly inch forward once more. As the scalpel penetrates the stomach which is, they note, peculiarly inflamed, a slimy reddish-brown liquid is released, similar, Mr Powell realises with deep misgiving, to the potion he has so recently prescribed. As Bucknill catches up some of it in a phial and secures the stopper, they all feel a sharp tang in their throats and on their tongues. Stepping back from the tomb, he loosens his mask and addresses his colleagues:

> 'I trust, gentlemen, that you agree that there is no need to prolong this investigation further.'

And as they nod in relieved agreement, he turns to the Coroner. 'Mr Fox, you may now proceed with the Inquest. However, without wishing in any way to pre-empt your conclusions, in my humble opinion you cannot help but find that the death of this unfortunate young man has been brought about by most unnatural means – at the hand, it is only proper to add, of person or persons unknown.'

Unknown perhaps, but all eyes turn to the man standing expressionless on the fringe of the family group: John Donellan, Captain in the service of His Gracious Majesty's British East India Company (cashiered), Master of the Ceremonies at the Pantheon Pleasure Palace, London (bankrupted) and husband of Theodosia, sister of Sir Theodosius – and his sole heir.

Chapter One

JOHN DONELLAN. He was born in Ireland on 6th November 1737. The Donnellans (they wavered between the double and single 'n') had a record of long and distinguished public service in that country. His great-grandfather, Nehemiah, was Lord Chief Baron of the Exchequer and his father, also Nehemiah, was, like many in the family, a military man – a Lieutenant Colonel who commanded the 39th Regiment of Foot. He saw active service in the War of Austrian Succession and was wounded in 1745 at the Battle of Fontenoy where the combined British, Austrian and Dutch forces were defeated by the French.

John is another recurring Donnellan name, but at some stage an attempt has been made to expunge all mention of him from the family archives. Part of the entry relating to his father has been deleted, but it is still possible to read that 'he was not married but he had an illegitimate son John whom he treats as an ordinary son.'

His mother is also missing from the records but Nehemiah did indeed oversee his son's upbringing and arranged his entry at the age of fourteen into the Royal Military Academy in Woolwich. After serving as a Cadet in the Royal Artillery he volunteered to serve in India, where the British were engaged in a struggle for supremacy with the old enemy, the French, and in 1757 he was posted to Madras as a Subaltern in his father's former regiment. Shortly afterwards though the corps was ordered back to England but Donellan, along with several fellow officers, opted to remain behind in the service of the East India Company.

In December 1757, armed with recommendations from his commanding officer, Colonel Lawrence, and George Pigot, the Governor of Madras, he received a commission as Captain and set about recruiting other members of the departing force. His zeal was acknowledged by Robert Clive himself, who in a letter to Donellan, declared that he was 'very glad you have had such success in raising so many men out of the poor remains of his Majesty's detachments sent to Bengal. I need not tell you that, exclusive of Mr Pigot and Colonel Lawrence's recommendation, your own merits will entitle you to all the services in my power.'

Donellan's company was commanded by Colonel Francis Forde who in late 1758 embarked on a campaign to drive the French out of the state of Golconda. On 14th December, whilst engaged in a skirmish at Chumbole, Donellan was hit in the leg by a musket ball. He was transported forty miles to a Dutch factory on the coast where better medical facilities were available and the injury was sufficiently serious for the surgeons to contemplate amputation. However, he fought against this and, with the wound still open and unable to walk without crutches, he insisted on rejoining his comrades as they prepared to lay siege to the state's capital, Mazulipatum.

This was a pivotal moment in the entire campaign and years later Donellan was to give a vivid account of what he claimed was his particular role in the affair. The siege had already dragged on for several weeks when, at ten o'clock on the night of 7th April, the British launched an all-out assault.

As they drove the defenders back from their entrenched positions, Donellan saw that Colonel Forde was held up on the far side of a deep ditch. Removing his sash, he threw one end over the gap and hauled his commander across. There is unfortunately no corroborating evidence for this action but whilst modestly protesting that it was not becoming 'to insist on the merit of his services', Donellan goes on to tell how he then embarked on an even greater exploit.

Conscious that the British were heavily outnumbered, he offered to enter the town in secret and alone, apart from his sergeant who, as a deserter from the French side, 'knew every quarter of the town.' If, he declared, he could take the Governor, the Marquis de Conslans, prisoner, surrender would quickly follow. Forde was very doubtful that this 'rash and impracticable' plan would work but allowed himself to be persuaded.

Under cover of darkness, the two men passed through the gate of the arsenal, even though this was guarded by a file of musketeers with bayonets fixed. A twelve-pounder cannon 'was pointed towards the street; which a soldier with a lighted match stood prepared to discharge on the first approach of an enemy.' Taking advantage of the general confusion brought on by the British assault, Donellan penetrated the Governor's apartment and swiftly convinced him that further resistance was futile. Nothing but 'immediate surrender could prevent all the dreadful consequences of a storm.' Faced with this ultimatum, the Marquis immediately gave in and Donellan, accompanied by a French officer, returned to his own force, his mission safely accomplished.

He ends his account with the pious thought that 'thus the reduction of this place was achieved with little or no loss to the besiegers, and without that carnage, so horrible to humanity, too often the unavoidable consequence of a place's being taken by assault.' Unfortunately, however, the two contemporary accounts of the siege make no mention of his role. In both, de Conslans made the first move, sending one of his officers with an offer to surrender if honourable terms could be agreed. In response, Forde despatched one of his captains with the threat that unless all hostile fire ceased immediately he would be obliged 'to put the whole garrison to the sword.'

Donellan might of course have been the anonymous 'captain' but even so, in these versions his act of derring-do has been reduced to that of a mere message carrier. Although his account appears then to be sheer fantasy, it is possible that the omission of his heroic deeds from the 'authorised' accounts was engineered by Forde who would not of course have wanted his own role to be portrayed in such a secondary, not to say, inadequate fashion. Whatever the truth of the matter, Donellan was in any case very shortly to fall foul of his commanding officer.

Before the siege had even begun, the British had agreed among themselves that agents should be chosen from within their ranks to secure any spoils. As soon as the surrender was confirmed, four men were duly appointed, with Donellan as the senior officer in charge. They set about their task with enthusiasm and had soon appropriated for their own personal benefit a large amount of booty, most of it coming from the Indian merchants in the town.

Learning of this, Forde ordered that such property should be returned without delay. This was not at all what Donellan and his companions had in mind and they interpreted the instruction as requiring the merchants to pay them an equivalent amount of the items' worth before they could regain their own possessions. Furthermore, these transactions could be accomplished much more readily on receipt of additional 'considerations'.

Donellan was later to claim that Forde had been given a totally false impression of the transactions by his steward, a Banyan named Tymany, going so far as to drop dark hints about the nature of their relationship. However, on 28th April 1759 all four men were brought before a court-martial presided over by the Governor and Council of Bengal.

Donellan argued that as agents for the East India Company they had been acting in a civil capacity and should not therefore have to face a military trial. He also declared that the payments they had received (some fifty pounds each) had been 'spontaneously presented' by the merchants in gratitude for their 'alacrity' in returning the goods. In any case, he asserted, most of the so-called merchants were in fact Frenchmen in disguise, with many of the items bearing the cypher of the French East India Company.

But all of these arguments were brushed aside and there followed a procession of aggrieved witnesses claiming that even though they had paid the bribes demanded of them much of their property had still not been returned. An Armenian merchant, Maurood Sarkise, gave a vivid account of his dealings with the accused:

> 'The gentlemen to whom he applied for the delivery of his goods which had been ordered to be given to him took from his house a hand-scrutore, with money and jewels in it, and, upon applying to have it returned, was refused, except he would give some money, which he at last consented to do, and paid the prisoner, Captain John Donnellan, one thousand rupees, and had the scrutore returned to him, but missed one or two large emeralds, and two or three small ones.' When he complained, 'Captain Donnellan showed him one of the large ones, which was lying among the other things, and told him, as for the others, some of the other gentlemen had taken them to make rings or buttons of.'

After a hearing lasting two days, during which the accused had been allowed to cross-examine the witnesses and to speak in their own defence (neither of which was permitted at this time in a civil court) all four were found guilty and dismissed the service with ignominy.

Chapter Two

FOLLOWING THE verdicts, Donellan's three comrades in arms, all of whom had tried to pin the blame on him as the instigator of their actions, confessed their guilt and were immediately reinstated but he refused to follow their craven example. He was though determined to remain in India and was – or so he was to claim later – approached by de Conslans who made 'many tempting offers … with a view to engage him in the service of France.' But he never for one moment forgot 'his duty to the Company, or his allegiance to his natural Sovereign.'

Learning of plans for a fresh campaign out of Bengal to be led by Colonel Forde, he immediately offered his services. Presumably he thought that his exploits at Mazulipatum would negate his recent problems but his former commanding officer seems to have quite forgotten both those gallant deeds and his personal indebtedness. On the other hand, Forde had neither forgotten nor forgiven certain remarks which Donellan optimistically assumed had not reached his ears.

In a letter dated 17th November 1759, which despite being addressed to 'Captain John Donnellan', for he had retained his military rank, and concluding with the conventional 'I am, Sir, your most humble servant', Forde makes no attempt to hide his feelings:

> Sir,
> I have just received your note, wherein you offer to attend me in whatever capacity I shall think proper to employ you. I must say, it surprised me not a little that you would deign to serve under a man whose character you made so free with in all companies in this town; especially as you were pleased to say I know nothing of my profession, and you would break a lance corporal who was not capable of making

a better disposition than I made at the action near Peddepore. I must beg
therefore to be excused from accepting your proposal.

Unabashed, Donellan continued attempting to persuade the East India Company
to overturn his conviction but he finally accepted the inevitable and returned to
England. He still had not given up on the military entirely but his efforts to
purchase a commission in the Cavalry were thwarted. He needed a certificate of
good behaviour from the Company and Forde, still grinding his personal axe,
constantly blocked this.

He went above their heads, appealing to Robert (now Lord) Clive, both in
writing and calling on him at his London residence. But beyond confirming his
opinion of Donellan as a courageous officer he was unable to help. There is a
certain irony here for Clive, in his wayward youth in his home town of Market
Drayton in Shropshire, had organised a racket of his own extorting protection
money from the local shopkeepers. And questions were being asked about the
sources of his personal wealth, for whilst Governor of Bengal he had accepted
lavish gifts from Indian rulers he had supported or helped into power. These far
outstripped the pickings that Donellan had allegedly obtained and although a
parliamentary enquiry of 1772-3 cleared him, his reputation was tainted and in
1774 he committed suicide.

Misfortunes of another kind awaited Donellan in England. In 1762 Anne
Donellan of Charles Street, Berkeley Square, patron of the arts, personal friend of
Handel, made an amendment to her will. The bequest intended for her nephew
Nehemiah was to go instead to his son, Captain John Donellan, 'lately returned
from the Indies.' This change was made because the previous year Nehemiah had
been certified insane.

It is not clear whether this was the culmination of growing instability or whether
it was the disgrace which his son had brought on both the family and his old
regiment that pushed him over the edge. He was confined to a madhouse but when
Donellan learnt of this he successfully applied to the Court of King's Bench for a
writ of Habeas Corpus. He was removed to his native Ireland, where he lived for
over twenty years in happy ignorance of the tragic events that were soon to engulf
his son.

A legacy was one thing but Donellan's great-aunt showed no sign of imminent
demise. And in any case, his was just one bequest among many. As well as leaving
her portrait of Handel to the newly-established British Museum, she had instructed

that her house in one of the most fashionable addresses in London should be sold to enhance her estate. But this was to be shared among numerous cousins, nieces and nephews, as well as such good causes as the promotion of 'religion, learning and good manners.'

Donellan therefore was forced to look around for other employment, and three years after his return, he finally received the good conduct certificate. This was couched in very guarded terms, making no mention of the court martial and acknowledging that he had conducted himself as a 'gallant officer', but although doubtless grateful for the Captain's half pay for which he was now eligible he had by then lost interest in renewing his army career.

He had for some time cut a dashing figure in the salons and gaming houses of London's demi-monde. We hear of him, for example, in 1770 devising the entertainments at the soirées hosted by Mrs Cornely, one of the most prominent socialites of the time, at her house in Soho Square. Her Assembly Rooms were the most fashionable private venue in London, featuring balls, masquerades and other entertainments. The eight-year old Mozart performed there in 1764, and Goldsmith's comedy of manners *She Stoops to Conquer* was presented in February 1773, a month before its official premiere at Covent Garden.

Donellan had acquired the nickname 'Ring Donellan' on account of the diamond ring he habitually wore. Although the largest gem Maurood Sarkise complained of losing was an emerald, this is suspiciously reminiscent of the defrauded merchant's property. However, as his financial worries – particularly his gambling debts – increased, Donellan was forced to dispose of it, but the sale was transacted in the strictest secrecy and a paste copy saved him from losing face among his peers.

He formed liaisons with several of the ladies in their circle, including at least one married woman who placed her servants and carriage at his disposal, but these affairs, though no doubt pleasurable, were all short-lived. But then, in January 1772, he was appointed to what must have seemed to him the dream post of Master of the Ceremonies at the newly opened Pantheon Pleasure Palace.

This had been conceived as a winter equivalent of the Ranelagh Gardens, providing an indoor place of entertainment for the aristocracy and their hangers-on, its season running from December to May. It was the first major commission of James Wyatt, who was just twenty-six and was to go on to rival Robert Adam as the leading architect of the age. It stood on the south side of Oxford Street on the site now occupied by Marks and Spencer.

Bidding to emulate if not outshine Ranelagh's rococo rotunda, the centre-piece was a large circular space modelled on the church of Saint Sophia in Constantinople, with its plaster dome an exact replica of the one in the original Pantheon in Rome. Beneath this was the tea and supper room, whilst leading off it was a series of corridors linking smaller rooms for card games and other pursuits. The building aroused universal admiration. For Horace Walpole it was 'the most beautiful edifice in England' whilst Dr Burney went even further, declaring that it was 'regarded both by nationals and foreigners as the most elegant structure in Europe, if not the world.'

To finance the scheme shares were sold at £600 each and one of these was bought by Donellan. It is unclear how he managed to raise such a large sum (not far short of forty thousand pounds in today's terms), but it was an essential prerequisite of the Master of the Ceremonies that he should have a financial interest in the enterprise. He could well have gained the appointment through his acquaintance with Miss Margareth Ellice. A prominent figure in London society, she was a substantial backer of the project, purchasing thirty of the original fifty shares. She had previously played a leading part in planning and conducting the entertainments for Mrs Cornely and thus had first-hand knowledge of Donellan's expertise in such matters. (It was also through her influence that Mrs Cornely herself invested heavily in the venture.)

The Pantheon opened to great acclaim on 27th January 1772, with among the guests all the foreign ambassadors, the Lord Chancellor, Lord North, and numerous other members of the nobility, including Clive. Conscious of the reputation that Ranelagh had gained as a venue for licentious behaviour, it was decreed that ladies could gain admission only on 'the recommendation of a peeress.'

Such a requirement proved hopelessly impractical but even so Donellan soon 'found himself greatly embarrassed to execute his office on account of the rigour with which ladies of easy virtue were exempted from admission.' He had to tread a very delicate path but even so frequently fell foul of patrons who found their would-be companions barred. Several frustrated gallants went so far as to seek satisfaction in the form of duels but each time he managed to smooth their ruffled feathers before such a drastic resolution actually materialised.

At first, the rotunda was used simply for assemblies, with the emphasis on the patrons seeing and being seen. After James Boswell and Dr Johnson had made what had quickly become the obligatory visit, Boswell remarked that 'there was not half a guinea's worth of pleasure in seeing this place', to which Johnson retorted,

'But, sir, there is half a guinea's worth of inferiority to other people in not having seen it.' Boswell though was not convinced. 'I doubt, sir,' he declared, 'whether there are many happy people here.' But his companion disagreed. 'Yes, sir, there are many happy people here. There are many people here who are watching hundreds, and who think hundreds are watching them.'

However, this austere regime was soon abandoned. Subscription concerts followed by dancing were arranged and each season, following Ranelagh's example and with Donellan drawing on the experience he had gained at Mrs Cornely's, at least two elaborate masquerades were staged. These, in particular, with their Venetian-style masked balls provided numerous opportunities for sexual intrigue.

With the exception of the aggrieved young bloods, it was generally agreed that Donellan was making a success of his role. He was though falling into increasing financial difficulties. With a combination of gambling losses and generally living beyond his means, his debts were building up at an alarming rate. According to one account, he found himself confined in a sponging house, a sort of halfway house on the road to the Bridewell Prison, and from where he could only be released on payment of his debts. He was thus forced to sell, at a greatly reduced price, his share in the Pantheon and this in turn led to the loss of his position there.

For someone in his situation (and with the bench-mark of his fortieth birthday rapidly approaching) there was one obvious remedy – marry an heiress. And it was at this low ebb in his fortunes that his path was crossed by the Dowager Lady Boughton and her nineteen-year old daughter, Theodosia.

Chapter Three

LADY ANNA Maria Beauchamp Boughton was a member, as her name suggests, of the notable Beauchamp family. She herself was an heiress when she married Sir Edward Boughton, sixth baronet, of Little Lawford in Warwickshire. The baronetcy dated from 1641 and the Boughtons were one of the most prominent and wealthy families in the county.

It was his second marriage, the first – much against his family's wishes – being to a Miss Anna Brydges from Somerset, who was some thirty years his senior. Unsurprisingly, she died childless but he and Lady Anna had two children: Theodosia, who was born on the 25th of May 1757 and, three years later, a son named with a singular lack of imagination Theodosius. Derived from the Greek, it means gift of God but, in the boy's case at least, this was to prove sadly inappropriate.

Sir Edward died of an 'apoplexy' (the usual term at this time for a stroke or seizure) in 1771 when his wife was still in her early thirties. The male Boughtons had a tendency to sudden deaths; Sir Edward's father, the fifth baronet and another Edward, died aged thirty-three of, it was said, 'intemperance'. The talk went further, with hints of insanity, and there were even accusations that his step-mother had encouraged his heavy drinking in order to bring about his death so that her own son might inherit. Although this was hotly disputed, it was widely agreed that he was apt 'to be whimsical when in his cups.'

Under the terms of his father's will, Theodosius, just eleven years old when he inherited the title, would on his coming of age receive an income of two thousand pounds (over one hundred and twenty-five thousand in today's value). If he should die before the age of twenty-one, this would pass to his sister.

He was put under the guardianship of two family friends, Sir William Wheler and Sir Francis Skipwith, whilst Lady Boughton had sole charge of Theodosia. Sir

Francis died soon afterwards and although Sir William lived less than ten miles away in the hamlet of Leamington Hastings he seems to have been very much an absentee guardian, leaving both the running of the estate and the upbringing of both children to Lady Boughton. She was unfortunately a weak, vacuous woman who indulged their every whim and Theodosius in particular began to exhibit all the traits of what in a later age would be termed a 'spoilt brat.' By his mid-teens he was virtually ungovernable; he was removed from nearby Rugby School and sent to Eton but this, if anything, only gave further scope for his unruliness.

There are conflicting accounts of how Donellan entered their lives. There was possibly a family connection in that a relative of Sir Edward had married the first Lord Templeton of Ireland, and his sister was a Mrs Donnellan. But there were numerous Mrs Donnellans in Ireland at this time and the link seems tenuous to say the least.

Otherwise, we have two versions of their first meeting. In one, the fateful encounter took place in the Pantheon. Lady Boughton and her daughter had come up to town to sample the delights of the season but when they entered the far from hallowed portals of the pleasure palace the two country mice were quite overwhelmed by the brittle aura of the glitterati that surrounded them. They were therefore grateful for the assiduous attentions of the Director of Entertainments as he steered them through this alien world.

Lady Boughton was at least as captivated by his Irish charm as was Theodosia – they were, after all, much of an age – but Donellan's ambitions were of course focused on the daughter, who was already in possession of some three thousand pounds, with the promise of much more should her brother predecease her. But he was acutely aware that a cashiered, debt-ridden army officer on half pay, the illegitimate son of a lunatic father, was hardly ideal son-in-law material.

But Theodosia, naïve and wilful, revelled in the romance of the liaison with its smuggled letters and secret meetings and these culminated in June 1777 in that most enthralling of adventures, an elopement and clandestine marriage.

In the second version the scene moves from London to another gathering place of the rich and famous. Donellan, we are told, was in even more straitened circumstances and having lost his position at the Pantheon had moved to Bath where, at the height of the season, the meeting took place.

Lady Boughton and Theodosia, arriving in the late afternoon, found to their dismay that there were no rooms available at any of the hotels or inns. All that they were offered, at the last hostelry they tried, were two chairs in the sitting room. But

Donellan, who happened to be already staying in that very inn, overheard their plight and gallantly insisted that they take his room for the night. Overwhelmed with gratitude, the ladies invited him to join them at breakfast the next morning and matters proceeded from there.

Whichever version is correct – and the second seems even more apocryphal than the first – Lady Boughton was of course both mortified and outraged at its conclusion but before she could cut her daughter off without the proverbial penny Donellan took steps to persuade her that he was no mere fortune-hunter. Although at that time it was customary on marriage for a husband to take possession of all his wife's assets, Donellan anticipated by a century the Married Women's Property Act. He had a legal settlement drawn up whereby he not only debarred himself from any control over Theodosia's finances but also from possessing 'all or some part of his wife's fortune for his life after her decease.' He also made a will in which he stated that should he or his wife die without issue any property he did possess in his own right would pass to Theodosius.

In a further attempt to heal the rift he and Theodosia visited her brother at Eton, where they were horrified by what they found. The youth's waywardness had descended into debauchery and he was housed 'at a Mrs Roberts' there, in a deep salivation for the venereal disease, under the care of a Mr Pearson, surgeon of that place.'

The illness was inevitably ascribed to Theodosius's supposed life-style. Donellan was later to blame it on his 'intemperances and his unfortunate connections with different women.' But this might have been doing him an injustice for his illness could well have been inherited. The deaths of both his father and grandfather were linked to 'intemperance', and apoplexy and mental instability are among the more extreme symptoms of the disease. So it is quite possible that Lady Boughton had contracted it in its secondary form from her husband and passed this on to her son. Congenital syphilis is only transmitted through the male line, so Theodosia would have escaped any such misfortune.

Whatever the truth, Lady Boughton was informed of the youth's condition and she swiftly removed him from school, enlisted as private tutor a Mr Jones from Northampton and, on more personal matters, Mr Clare, a Rugby apothecary. Donellan and Theodosia had by now returned to Bath and she wrote to them there, updating them on his condition. His complexion had deteriorated for blotches had appeared on his face – and elsewhere on his body although, out of delicacy perhaps, she fails to mention this.

As a further step towards reconciliation Lady Boughton and Theodosius paid a visit to Bath. But this was not an unmitigated success for the young man's incorrigible nature led him into a series of unedifying quarrels, from which he was rescued by Donellan, no stranger to taking a firm hand with petulant youths.

The breach was finally healed in June 1778, by which time their first child, tactfully called Maria after one of Lady Boughton's forenames, had been born. The runaways were invited to stay at Lawford Hall and, with Theodosius still several years short of his majority and in any case incapable of managing his own affairs let alone anybody else's, his mother was at first happy for the visit to become permanent and for Donellan to take charge of the day to day running of the estate.

In *The Life of Capt John Donnellan*, published after his death in 1781, we learn that 'from this time no arrangement was made without his advice, nor alteration in the domestic economy admitted but with his participation. He directed every business according to his own ideas, and found obedience paid to his orders, as though he had been the owner of the mansion. In short, nothing could exceed the authority which he assumed, but the deference and submission with which his commands were received.'

Unsurprisingly, this did not go down well with the Hall servants, who deeply resented taking orders from this interloper. His unpopularity spread further when he prohibited the boys of Rugby School from following the long-established practice of fishing in the river Avon where it ran through the Hall's land. Although Donellan contemptuously brushed aside these little local difficulties they were going to prove crucial in the light of later events.

Sir William Wheler was well aware of Donellan's past history. His younger brother, Francis, had been a fellow officer with the East India Company while another brother, Edward, was a Director on the Board of the Company, the very body that Donellan had addressed in his appeal for reinstatement in the military. However, he kept his own counsel and the two men managed to maintain at least a veneer of civility towards each other.

Unlikely as it might seem, given his life-style up to this point, Donellan – at least by his own account – also began to take instruction to enter the priesthood. Following her husband's death, Lady Boughton had become patron of the neighbouring parishes of Harborough Magna and Newbold-on-Avon. But Donellan was to claim that Theodosius had grandly promised that when he came of age he would present him with the Harborough living and, once the present incumbent died – and he was, after all, in his seventies – with that of Newbold, both worth upwards of two hundred pounds a year.

This would have come as a nasty surprise to the two current incumbents who both, as was the norm at that time, regarded their posts as 'jobs for life'. The Reverend Peers Newsam had been at Harborough since 1772 and in fact remained there until his death in 1786, whilst John Parker enjoyed an even longer occupancy of Newbold, from 1742 to 1787, when he was succeeded, as he had long envisaged, by his son John.

Theodosius meanwhile showed no sign of reform and his hasty temper led him into further scrapes. He had taken to frequenting the Rugby Assembly Rooms and on two occasions – first with a Mr Wildgoose from Daventry then with a Rugby vicar, the Reverend Charters – the quarrels reached the pitch of his challenging them to duels. On each occasion he sent for his brother-in-law to act as his second but Donellan, using all his powers of tact and persuasion, managed to extricate him from these predicaments unharmed.

Theodosius had also developed a penchant for swimming in the large and very deep pond in the Hall grounds. There could have been an added attraction here for the pool was reputed to be the final resting place of the ghost of Lawford Hall. Every self-respecting country house needs its ancestral spectre and in the case of Lawford this was 'One-handed Boughton', who lived at the time of the first Elizabeth and was so-called because he had lost an arm. He was frequently to be seen driving a ghostly coach and six round the neighbourhood and was also reputed to haunt one of the Hall bedrooms, much to the terror of the maids.

By the middle of the eighteenth century his shenanigans were getting so out of hand that Sir Edward Boughton, Theodosius' father, called on the Reverend Thomas Hall, the then rector of Harborough Magna, to exorcise him. This he did, in the company, it was said, of eleven other clergymen, all solemnly carrying lighted candles. The unruly spirit was caught in a glass phial and thrown into the estate's flooded marl pit. Shortly afterwards Sir Edward was strolling in the Hall grounds with Sir Francis Skipwith when the latter remarked that there must be a great many fish in the pool and he would like to try for some, but Sir Edward replied in all seriousness, 'No, that I cannot consent to, for the spirit of my ancestor, the One-handed Boughton, lies there.'

Apart from the pool's depth, the danger was increased by the reeds and bullrushes growing there but Theodosius ignored all Donellan's warnings. In the end an exasperated Donellan enlisted the help of the gardener to literally pull the plug on these activities by raising the bolt in the pool bottom to at least ensure that the reckless youth stayed within his depth.

On yet another occasion, Donellan saved him from an even greater act of folly. The two of them, together with Lady Boughton, were paying a visit to John Parker, the rector of Newbold, blissfully unaware of the succession plans being hatched by two of his guests. Theodosius, always easily bored, took it into his head to take the key to the church and climb the stairs up to the battlemented tower. Donellan, wondering what he was going to get up to this time, went with him and his fears were realised when the young man announced that he was going to shin up the pole that surmounted the tower to the weathercock and turn it.

Despite Donellan's protests he began the ascent and had just reached the top when his foot slipped and he fell heavily into his brother-in-law's waiting arms. The impact was so great that Donellan was violently sick and in the coach going back to the Hall Theodosius grudgingly admitted that his presence of mind had probably saved his life.

Donellan was growing increasingly exasperated with these antics for other, more pressing, matters were occupying his mind. A second daughter, Theodosia King, was born in July 1779. She was though a sickly infant and on 20th October that same year her tiny coffin was laid in the family crypt in Newbold church.

By then, however, Theodosia was pregnant again and on 21st July 1780 there was a far happier ceremony at Newbold when 'John Donnellan, Son of John Donnellan Esq & Theodosia Beauchamp his Wife' was baptised. This will have come as a welcome respite for Lady Boughton, whose concerns about her son were now centred round his intentions regarding a local beauty, a certain Miss Fonnereau. Fully aware of his physical condition, which was showing no sign of improvement, and perhaps conscious of her own experience, she had done her best to discourage any talk of marriage but her alarm increased when Theodosius invited the young lady's brother to stay at the Hall, with the intention of returning home with him. She seems to have been alone in thinking that matters had reached such a stage but knowing her son's impetuous nature she confided in Donellan, asking him to reinforce her attempts to deter him. But the youth was by now refusing to take advice from his brother-in-law or anyone else.

Whatever might have been in his mind though would, in any case, come to nothing for just six weeks after the christening, at the very time of the proposed visit, the family gathered once more at Newbold church and the crypt was reopened, this time to receive the body of the unhappy young man.

Chapter Four

THEODOSIUS'S HEALTH had been causing increasing concern for some time. After his removal from Eton he lived for five months at the home near Northampton of Mr Jones, the private tutor his mother had chosen for him. On his return to Lawford Hall, Donellan was shocked by the change in both 'his countenance and person.'

Suspecting that he 'had contracted a fresh venereal complaint' (although in fact it could have been the existing condition reasserting itself) he questioned him privately and after at first refusing to respond, the youth finally admitted that he was indeed suffering from 'his old complaint'. His lower body was covered in open, weeping sores and whilst in the Jones's household he had taken to wearing 'flannel drawers every night, in order to prevent a discovery upon the sheets'. He had also been applying 'a great deal of mercurial ointment', for since at least the early sixteenth century, mercury had been regarded as a cure for the disease, recommended by such figures as Paracelsus, the Swiss scientist and medical pioneer.

Donellan confided in Lady Boughton but instead of placing her son under the care of a fully qualified medical man, as he advised, she merely gave Theodosius a copy of 'The Family Physician'. This was a do-it-yourself manual published ten years previously with the sub-title 'A collection of useful family remedies', and from which, in Donellan's words, he was 'continually quacking himself'.

However, with no sign of improvement, Lady Boughton finally relented, and after briefly calling in two local practitioners, in June 1781 she put her son under the care of Thomas Powell, a Rugby apothecary. Although he was shocked to learn of his patient's amateur efforts, he continued the mercury treatment in the form of boluses or large soluble tablets of calomel.

The white crystalline powder was considered an effective purgative and Powell repeated the prescription regularly for three weeks then, after a fortnight's break, renewed it because Theodosius had developed a swelling in his groin. This time he added a cleansing embrocation together with draughts of manna and salts. The former was not the miraculous food of the Israelites but a sweet, solidified juice obtained by incisions in the stem of the ash tree and was used as a mild laxative or diuretic.

But during the weekend prior to his death Theodosius vomited several times so on the Monday the manna and salts were replaced by fifteen grains each of jalap (or bindweed) and rhubarb. Powell was clearly aiming to intensify the cleansing effect for the latter had been used as a purgative for centuries. (Macbeth, as his enemies close in on him, demands of the Doctor, 'What rhubarb, senna, or what purgative drug would scour these English hence?') In Theodosius's case it also had the attraction, according to Nicholas Culpepper, the seventeenth century alchemist and physician, of being 'very effectual to stay the running of the reins, or gonorrhoea.'

Not surprisingly, the youth was in a very low frame of mind, and the apothecary also added two drachms of nutmeg water and twenty drops of spirits of lavender, a common remedy for headaches and depression. This new concoction, at least according to Powell, 'purged him very well, and agreed with him very well; he had many stools.' Encouraged by this, on the Tuesday evening he sent a repeat prescription. But within twelve hours his patient was dead.

Suspicion at first centred inevitably on Powell's potions. As her son lay dying, Lady Boughton exclaimed to Donellan that 'it was an unaccountable thing in the doctor to send such a medicine, for if it had been taken by a dog it would have killed him.' The apothecary of course hotly disclaimed all responsibility, and also tried to play down the seriousness of the young man's illness. When he was first consulted, the venereal disease was 'rather slight, a fresh complaint' and the swelling in the groin was 'a very small one; it did not rise above the skin.'

This seems very much at odds with both Theodosius's medical history and Powell's own assiduous attentions – he called on his patient on both the Sunday and the Tuesday before his death. It also conflicts with the concerns expressed by Donellan and Lady Boughton and, of course, Theodosius himself, but the apothecary was clearly trying from the outset to attribute the death to foul play.

Similarly, after her initial reaction, Lady Boughton quickly transferred her suspicions to her son-in-law, and despite all the evidence she too attempted to give the impression that Theodosius had been essentially in good health. She declared that on both the night prior to his death and at first the following morning he 'seemed very well'.

Donellan on the other hand had expressed frequent concern about his brother-in-law's condition. When Lady Boughton mentioned to him that she was intending to be absent for a short while he strongly advised against this. 'Don't talk about leaving Lawford Hall; something or other may happen. He is in a very bad state of health.' And when on the Saturday before Theodosius's death the Revd Newsam, returning after a four-month absence, met Donellan at the Hall, he was told that the young man's health had worsened drastically.

In Donellan's view the mercury he was still taking, both inwardly and as a cream, was to blame. His blood was 'a mass of mercury and corruption' and in addition to the swelling in the groin 'his breath was so offensive they could hardly sit at table to eat with him.' His mind was also deteriorating so that 'his intellects at intervals were so much affected that nobody knew what it was to live with him.' Newsam's reaction was that if this were indeed the case he 'did not think his life was worth two years' purchase', to which Donellan replied gravely, 'Not one.'

However, as with so many of Donellan's assertions, there are conflicting accounts of this episode. He claimed that Newsam had already met Theodosius and began the conversation by commenting that the youth 'appeared much worse than usual.' The rector, on the other hand, declared that he had not, at this point, actually seen the baronet, and when he did the only change in his appearance was that his complexion was not so 'florid' as previously. As a man of the cloth, Newsam's version might seem the more likely but with his living dependent on the family's continuing favour, he would perhaps be more inclined to follow Lady Boughton's line.

Donellan claimed that his version was supported by a Mr Clay of Rugby, to whom Newsam had spoken a short time later, but this was never confirmed. In any case, his apparent concern is of course capable of two interpretations: it was either genuine and Powell and Lady Boughton were for their own reasons in retrospective denial, or he was cunningly preparing the ground for the execution of his murderous plot.

On the Tuesday afternoon the family dined as usual, between two and three o'clock, then went their separate ways. Mr Powell arrived to check on his patient and, encouraged by his apparent response to the amended prescription, made up another draught which Samuel Frost, 'Lady Boughton's serving boy', brought back to the Hall and handed directly to Theodosius.

At six, the lad followed the baronet down to the Avon, the river that flowed through the estate, to help him fish. Although the river is only a short distance from the house, Theodosius had gone there on horseback for his favoured tech-nique was to stay mounted, trawling the shallow stream with a net, with the young servant following him from the bank and holding the other end of the net.

At the same time, Lady Boughton and her daughter took a turn in the garden, strolling and chatting for over an hour. She was to claim later that she had seen nothing of Donellan since dinner but at about seven o'clock he came out of the house, saying that he had been down to the river and tried unsuccessfully to persuade Theodosius to come back with him, fearing that if he stayed much later he would catch cold.

Donellan flatly contradicted her story on all counts. He said that he was totally unaware of the delivery of the new potion for at the time he was walking in one of the Hall's fields with his two year-old daughter Maria. On his return, he saw Lady Boughton emerge from the house carrying a basket. She said she was going to pick fruit in the orchard and asked him to help her. He agreed and they were thus engaged when Theodosius rode past on his way to the river.

Samuel was not with him, and as some of the fruit was out of reach Lady Boughton asked Donellan to go back to the Hall and tell the boy to bring a ladder.

On his way into the house, he called 'Sam' several times but getting no response went into the kitchen where three female servants – Sarah Blundell, the housemaid, Susannah (more familiarly known as Sukey) Sparrow, his wife's maid, and the cook, Catherine Amos – were busy washing. They did not know where the lad was so he told them to track him down and send him out to the orchard. He was, he claimed, out of Lady Boughton's sight for no more than three minutes.

Samuel – and the ladder – duly appeared soon afterwards and then the young man went on down to the river to join Theodosius. The fruit picking though was broken off again when Sarah Blundell came out to tell Lady Boughton that a Mr Dand had arrived together with a carpenter, one Matthews from Long Lawford, and wished to speak with her on business.

Donellan, who by now was virtually running the estate, went with her and the four of them conferred for about ten minutes before the visitors went out into the inner courtyard and Donellan returned to the orchard. However, seeing them making for the stables, he remembered that he had another matter to discuss and called them to him. This second conversation took several minutes then Dand left and the other two men walked the short distance to Hewitt's watermill to look at some alterations that were being made there.

They continued along the river bank, without apparently seeing Theodosius, to check on the state of the floodgates then carried on walking until gone nine o'clock. By then, a heavy dew had fallen and Matthews set out for home while Donellan returned to the Hall. Lady Boughton, he claimed, was in the parlour looking out into the garden as he passed and he straightaway joined her there. She was growing anxious about Theodosius and annoyed that he had stayed out so late.

It was almost dark by then and candles would have to be lit – something that as a frugal keeper of the Hall's purse she deplored. Early to bed, early to rise seems to have been the maxim for the Lawford household for she and Donellan had arranged to go riding next morning, leaving soon after six, when it would be barely light.

Theodosia joined them and immediately began fussing over her husband because his shoes and socks were wet, but instead of changing them he drank his usual nightcap of a 'bason of milk' and went upstairs to bed. Within five minutes, Theodosia had followed him, still with no sign of her brother.

The two versions of these crucial hours are of course irreconcilable, with Lady Boughton and Donellan trying to establish totally conflicting scenarios. According to her, his whereabouts were unknown for most of the time, giving him ample opportunity to tamper with Theodosius's potion, which was usually placed on the mantelpiece in the outer room of his sleeping quarters. This had been done at Donellan's suggestion – which he did not deny – after one occasion when Theodosius forgot to take the mixture. It would catch his eye as he came into the room, but also of course put it within easy reach of anyone with malicious intentions.

Donellan, on the other hand, provides a virtual minute by minute account of his movements from the moment Powell's final mixture arrived. His version of events in India, during and after Mazulipatum, show how adept he was at putting the most favourable gloss on his conduct, but whereas his claims there were unsubstantiated, many of his assertions about these later events were backed up by witnesses.

Theodosia could have cleared up some of the discrepancies, but there is no indication that she confirmed either her mother's story of their evening stroll in the garden or her husband's account of his return to the Hall and retirement to bed. Catherine Amos also kept her own counsel regarding Donellan's apparent search for Samuel, wisely perhaps for Sukey Sparrow, who was later to be loud in her defence of Donellan, paid the penalty by losing her privileged position as

Theodosia's personal maid, being placed instead under the charge of Lady Boughton, who could keep a close eye on her future conduct. The third maid, Sarah Blundell, had her own preoccupations and in fact died a short time later, after giving birth to an illegitimate child.

More persuasively, the two workmen, Dand and Matthews, supported Donellan's story, confirming the various stages of their conversations which would take him from soon after seven o'clock right up to his return to the Hall at dusk. This was not a complete alibi for he still had ample time to meddle with the potion after Theodosius's departure for the river but it does cast serious doubt on Lady Boughton's reliability – she either had a very faulty memory or was so convinced of Donellan's guilt that she was prepared to lie to bring him to justice.

Theodosius did in fact come back soon after nine and after a light supper went straight to his room. As Lady Boughton followed him upstairs he called out to her, reminding her that she was to wake him in the morning at seven and give him his next dose of physic. He also asked her to let Samuel go 'a-fishing' with him again next day and as he was expecting his friend Fonnereau he would want the boy to fit new straps onto one of the nets.

But in the event, there would be no point in any of this for Sir Theodosius Boughton, seventh Baronet, of Lawford Parva in the county of Warwickshire, would never go 'a-fishing' again.

Chapter Five

NEXT MORNING, Donellan was up by daybreak but there was no sign of Lady Boughton. They were intending to ride several miles to a friend of hers to make enquiries about a servant girl she had in mind as a replacement for Sarah Blundell. So after walking about the garden and stable yard for some time he stood beneath her chamber and called up to her. She finally appeared at a window at the top of the stairs between her room and her son's and said that she was not ready and it might be better for him to ride alone.

William Frost, the coachman – and presumably father of young Samuel – was waiting in the yard with the two horses but Donellan told him there was a change of plan and he would take the mare, the faster of the two animals, and ride to Newnham Wells, three quarters of a mile away, to take the waters as treatment for the gout from which he suffered. (The spring at King's Newnham had long had a reputation for its health-giving powers, and a baths complex, with an elaborate mosaic floor, had been established there.)

Lady Boughton had said that she would not be ready for some time but this was an understatement for, although she said nothing to Donellan at this stage, she was extremely concerned about Theodosius. She had gone to him at seven as she had promised but he was already awake for Samuel Frost had roused him an hour earlier to ask where the net straps were. He told her that the new bottle of physic was, as usual, on the shelf above the fireplace in the outer room, along with another phial filled with liquid and an assortment of bottles and 'gallipots' containing the various 'household remedies' he was taking.

He also asked her to have a piece of cheese ready to remove the taste of the potion. Taking the bottle labelled 'Purging draught for Sir Theodosius Boughton', she poured the contents into a small white basin and was about to administer it when he saw that there was still some sediment at the bottom. So she poured it back into the bottle and shook it. As she did so, a few drops spilt on the table but she gave him the rest.

Pulling a face, he said it smelt and tasted very nauseous and she replied that to her it smelt very strongly of bitter almonds. He tried to chew the cheese but spat it out and complained that he did not think he could keep the medicine down. So she gave him a drink of water but after swilling it round in his mouth he spat this out as well then lay back quietly on the bed.

However, almost immediately a horrifying change took place. In Lady Boughton's own words, 'In two minutes, or a minute and a half, after he had taken it he struggled very much. He made a prodigious rattling in his stomach, and guggling, and he appeared to me to make very great efforts to keep it down.'

This went on for about ten minutes but then he seemed calmer and fell into a doze so she quietly left the room. It was at this point that she told Donellan there would be a slight delay but when, five minutes later, she went back to check on her son 'to my great surprise I found him with his eyes fixed upwards, his teeth clenched, and froth running out of each corner of his mouth.'

Rushing downstairs, she ran to the stables and told Frost to fetch Mr Powell as quickly as possible for her son was very sick. Her horse was ready saddled but, panicking now, she said it would not go fast enough and he should take the mare. Frost was on the point of saying it was not available when Donellan returned and the coachman 'out of breath and somewhat agitated', took the horse and galloped off towards Rugby.

Lady Boughton hurried back into the house, calling for the maids, and Donellan caught up with her, asking what had happened. She replied that something terrible had occurred and she very much feared her son was dying. Together, they raced up the stairs and into the bedroom, to find the young man in a very bad way. He was lying motionless, apart from the heaving of his stomach, there was more froth round his mouth and still the awful gurgling in his throat.

The two maids arrived and Catherine Amos knelt beside him to wipe away the froth, but it kept reappearing. Turning to the distraught mother, Donellan asked what it was she had given Theodosius and where the phial was. There then followed one of the most disputed episodes in the entire saga, with Lady Boughton and Donellan giving radically conflicting accounts of an event that was to prove crucial in sealing his fate.

He claimed that he snatched up the bottle she indicated and held it up to the light to see if any trace of the mixture remained. But there were no dregs visible so he poured no more than a teaspoonful of water into the phial, shook it and poured it into the small white basin. Dipping in his finger, he tasted it several times but there was not enough to tell exactly what the potion contained. However, from what little he could taste, it seemed 'rather nauseous'.

It was though from this moment that Lady Boughton's fears that the calamity was caused by a tragic error on Mr Powell's part changed to suspicions that he was the victim of a cold-blooded murder attempt by Donellan. And as, over the next few days and weeks, her doubts hardened into certainty, she grew ever more determined to paint a picture of his behaviour here as damning proof of his guilt. Unfortunately, however, although she told her story under oath on three separate occasions, there were crucial differences each time as they became increasingly hostile to Donellan.

Because of an interruption to the Inquest, which was never satisfactorily explained, she gave her testimony before the Coroner twice. The first version is very close to Donellan's account. She gave him the bottle and 'he then put water into the bottle, and poured it and the settling of the bottle out together; put his finger into it, and informed this examinant it had a nauseous taste.' But repeating her evidence five days later she claimed that 'he did not taste the liquid at all, and threw the entire contents onto the floor.'

Six months later, at Donellan's trial at Warwick Assize, the scene had been embellished still further. Now, she alleged, he put enough water into the bottle to rinse it thoroughly then poured it away into a hand-wash basin which already contained dirty water. 'What are you at?' she exclaimed – or said she did. 'You should not meddle with the bottle.'

Without replying, he took a second phial from the mantelshelf, poured water into it, shook it then put some on his finger and tasted it. 'What are you about?' she demanded again. 'You ought not to meddle with the bottles.' To which he supposedly responded that he was simply tasting it – something that he had not done with the first bottle. The fact that none of these details was disclosed to the Coroner makes them highly suspect, but even so their narration at the trial was a major factor in establishing Donellan's guilt.

With Theodosius in his death throes, Sarah Blundell, bizarrely, began to clear the room. Lady Boughton later claimed that it was Donellan who ordered her to remove the white basin and the close-stool, which was giving off a foul stench, then gave her the empty medicine bottles. She said that she took these from the maid and set them back on the mantelshelf, telling her to leave them alone.

Then, according to her, Donellan told the girl to throw Theodosius's clothes into an inner room, adding that the stockings were still damp and that he must have caught his death of cold. She claimed that she examined the stockings and could find no sign of their having been wet. Then, with her attention back on her son, he thrust the bottles into the maid's hands again, telling her angrily to remove them. Lady Boughton made no mention of this at the Inquest and admitted later that she did not actually hear Donellan say this or see who took the phials from the room but she claimed that the maid had told her that this was what had happened. However, with Sarah Blundell by this time dead there was no way of confirming her story.

Donellan gave his customary far more innocuous account of all this. He said that it was Lady Boughton who began to remove her son's belongings, taking them into the dressing room. With the young man still alive – just – at this point, this seems barely credible unless in her distraught state she was seeking relief in action of any kind. Donellan, ever the attentive son-in-law, told the maid to help her mistress, ordering her in particular to remove the close-stool.

Then, 'happening at the time she was taking away the things to stand near the chimney-piece, where the chief part of the bottles stood, and seeing Sarah Blundell coming up to take them away, put some of them into her apron, and which was nothing more than anyone else might have very innocently done.'

All this while, Catherine Amos was kneeling by Theodosius, wiping away the froth that continued to bubble from his lips. But then, with one final violent convulsion, he died.

His sister, still ensconced in her rooms at the far end of the house with baby John, remained serenely unaware of these events until Donellan came to break the news to her. They were in the parlour when Lady Boughton arrived, just in time to hear Donellan telling Theodosia about the incident with the medicine bottles and her mother's reaction to this. He repeated his claim that he added water to them merely to try and discover what was in the potion, then sent for William Frost, the coachman, who was by now back from alerting Mr Powell.

'Will,' he said, 'don't you remember that I set out of the iron gates this morning about seven o'clock?'

'Yes, sir.'

'And that was the first time of my going out? I have never been on the other side of the house this morning. You remember that I set out there at seven o'clock this morning and asked for a horse to go to the Wells?'

'Yes, sir.'

'Then you are my evidence.'

'Yes, sir.'

Frost confirmed this but was not sure whether the exchange took place at this time or a day or two later. Donellan's need to establish an alibi for himself was in itself suspicious but, even if this conversation did take place within minutes of Theodosius's death, he was already conscious of Lady Boughton's growing hostility. But in any case, although it seemed to clear him of any nefarious actions that morning, he had had ample opportunity to tamper with the potion the previous day.

Mr Powell arrived post-haste before nine o'clock. He was met in the courtyard by Donellan who told him that Theodosius had died 'in convulsions', perhaps brought on by a chill. The two men hurried upstairs but by then of course the apothecary's patient was beyond all medical care.

Chapter Six

LADY BOUGHTON turned at once to practicalities. She sent for the individuals concerned with the preliminary arrangements for the funeral, including the Revd Parker, and by ten o'clock, while she was still at breakfast, this had been set for the following Monday, September 4th.

Donellan's exchange with the coachman seems to have allayed her suspicions, in the short term at least, for later that morning she called him into the 'great parlour', where she had some favours to ask of him. Among her son's properties was a farm rented by Thomas Parsons, and she would be grateful if she could take over the lease. Technically, as his heir, such powers had passed to his sister, but she was sure that Theodosia would consent to any proposal that Donellan might put to her. Also, she asked for his agreement (again on behalf of his wife) that a young relative of hers, a clergyman named Rye, should have the reversion of the living of Newbold on the death of Mr Parker. She was apparently unaware that her son had, if Donellan is to be believed, promised this to him, but the episode certainly seems to confirm Lady Boughton's recognition of his greatly enhanced authority in the family's affairs.

Even more strikingly, she then – at least according to Donellan – said that for some time past she had been considering changes to the marriage settlement, drawn up in the immediate aftermath of the elopement and which heavily favoured Theodosia. She had asked Mr Smith, an attorney in Northampton, to draw up a new deed, adding that she had discussed the matter with Sir William Wheler. It seems extraordinary that she should concern herself with such matters at this time, but it was perhaps her way of coping with her distress.

Next, she entrusted Donellan with writing to Sir William on her behalf, informing him of the death of his ward, and he immediately set about this task and the letter was taken across to Leamington Hastings by William Frost.

Dear Sir,

I am very sorry to be the communicator of Sir Theodosius's death to you, which happened this morning; he has been for some time past under the care of Mr Powell, of Rugby, for a similar complaint to that which he had at Eton. Lady Boughton and my wife are inconsolable; they join me in best respects to Lady Wheler, yourself, and Mr and Mrs Sitwell. We are much concerned to hear of their loss.

 I am, dear Sir, with the greatest esteem,

  Your most obedient servant,

  John Donellan

 Lawford Hall, Aug. 30, 1780

 To Sir William Wheler, Bart

As a bare statement of fact, the letter is unexceptionable, except of course that there is no mention of the instantaneous reaction to the final draught or any of the other horrifying details of the death-scene. Sir William did not receive the letter until two days later, on his return from Stanby in Derbyshire after attending the funeral of the new-born child of his daughter, Lucy Sitwell.

News of this second tragedy did not reach him then until the Friday, by which time gossip about the nature of Theodosius's death – and the first hints of poison – was already beginning to circulate. However, because this was no more than 'a flying report round the country', Sir William in his reply to Donellan's note makes no reference to it, apart from saying that 'the sudden and very untimely death of my poor unfortunate ward gives me great concern.' He then goes on to express in conventional terms his condolences to Lady Boughton and the rest of the family, promising that 'at a proper time I shall make my respects to them and you in person.'

However, the following day, Sunday, the Revd Newsam called on him, bearing a letter he had received from another member of the local gentry, Lord Denbeigh of Monks Kirby, which lies midway between Little Lawford and Coventry. Greatly alarmed by its contents, next morning – the day set for the funeral – Sir William wrote again to Donellan:

Lemington, Sept. 4, 1780

Dear Sir,

Since I wrote to you last, I have been applied to, as the guardian of the late Sir Theodosius Boughton, to enquire into the cause of his sudden death; and report says, that he was better the morning of his death, and before he took the physick, than he had been for many weeks, and that he was taken ill in less than half an hour, and died in two hours after he had swallowed the physick. Supposing this to be true, there is great reason to believe that the physick was improper, and that it might be the cause of his death: as it makes a great noise in the country, and as I find that I am very much blamed for not making some enquiry into the affair, I thought it necessary to call upon Mr Powell to give an account in what state of health he was in at the time of his death. I expect Mr Powell here every moment; his character is at stake; and I dare say it will be a great satisfaction to him to have the body opened, and though it is very late to do it now, yet it will appear from the stomach, whether there is any corrosive in it. As a friend to you, I must say that it will be a great satisfaction to me, and I am sure it must be to you, Lady Boughton and Mrs Donellan, when I assure you that it is reported, all over the country, that he was killed either by medicine or by poison. The country will never be convinced to the contrary unless the body is opened, and we shall be all very much blamed: therefore I must request it of you and the family, that the body may be immediately opened by Mr Wilmer, of Coventry, or Mr Snow, of Southam, in the presence of Dr Rattray, or any other physician that you and the family think proper.

Mr Powell is now with me, and from his account it does not appear that his medicines could be the cause of his death: he has not given him any mercury since June, and the physick that he took the morning of his death was composed of rhubarb and jalap, two very innocent drugs. Mr Powell says it will be a great satisfaction to him to have the body opened; and, for the above reasons, I sincerely wish it, as no reflection can be cast upon me, Lady Boughton, or you, if it is done; if it is not, we shall be much blamed. I will only add, that this affair makes me very unhappy, as it must do you, Lady Boughton, and Mrs Donellan. I beg of you to lay this affair before Lady Boughton, in as tender a manner as you can, and to point out to her the real necessity of complying with my request, and to say that it is expected by the country. I am, with respect to Lady Boughton, yourself, and Mrs Donellan,

Your sincere friend, and obliged humble servant,

Wm. Wheler

To John Donellan, Esq. Lawford Hall

The letter was delivered personally by Powell and, although we can only guess at the impact it had on Donellan, he replied at once:

Dear Sir,

I this moment received a letter from you, by Mr Powell, which I communicated to Lady Boughton and my wife, and we most cheerfully wish to have the body of Sir Theodosius opened for the general satisfaction, and the sooner it is done the better; therefore I wish you could be here at the time.

I am, dear Sir, with the greatest sincerity, your most obedient humble servant,

John Donellan
Lawford Hall, Sept. 4, 1780
To Sir William Wheler, Bart

Sir William's response was immediate:

Dear Sir,

I have this moment received the favour of your letter, and I am very happy to find that Lady Boughton, Mrs Donellan, and yourself, approve of having the body opened. I should wish to show Lady Boughton and every part of her family every respect that is in my power, but it would be very improper for me, or indeed any other person, except the faculty, to attend upon this occasion. One surgeon, a physician, and Mr Powell should attend as soon as possible. I hope that you understand that it is not to satisfy curiosity, but the publick, that I wished to have this done, and to prevent the world from blaming any of us, that had anything to do with poor Sir Theodosius.

I am, with great sincerity, your humble servant,

William Wheler
To John Donellan, Esq. Lawford Hall

Before even receiving this, Donellan had on his own initiative sent for the estate's plumber to unsolder the coffin and contacted Mr Bradford Wilmer, a surgeon, who would perform the autopsy, and Dr David Rattray, whose task was to examine in particular the contents of the stomach. They both practised in Coventry, but although this is only ten miles from Little Lawford, no word had reached them of the possibility of poison as the cause of death.

Mr Wilmer was out of town when the summons came, and it was dark by the time they reached the Hall, each in a post-chaise. Wilmer had with him a young assistant but he did not deign to introduce him to Donellan, who was waiting for them, candle in hand. He ushered them into the parlour where he asked if they had been contacted by or seen Sir William as he was expecting him to be present, but they replied that they had heard nothing from him.

The three men took some light refreshment while the coffin was being opened then, as they went back into the entrance hall, they met Mr Powell who was standing by a table reading a letter. It was clearly addressed to Donellan but the apothecary had opened it 'by accident' – or so he claimed. This was the second of Sir William's letters sent that day and after scanning it through Donellan passed it to the two doctors.

As they were reading it, he said that he had received an earlier note from the baronet but, fumbling in his waistcoat pocket, he simply produced the envelope. This of course was the letter in which the suspicions of poison were given as the prime reason for the autopsy, so the two Coventry men remained unaware of this.

Leaving their host in the hall, the medical men carried on upstairs to Theodosius's quarters. Wilmer was the first to go into the room where the opened coffin lay but within just a few seconds he had beaten a hasty retreat. The late summer heatwave was at its height and in the confines of the room the stench from the corpse was almost unbearable. Rattray then ventured in but when he saw a maggot crawling across the bloated, blackened face he too rapidly withdrew.

Back on the landing, the two men conferred and agreed that because of the high temperatures – which had continued throughout the five days since Theodosius's death – the body had already reached such a state of putrefaction that no useful purpose could be served in investigating further.

They were both to insist later that had they been aware of the rumours of poison they would have proceeded but when back downstairs they asked Donellan why an autopsy had been requested he blandly – and in direct contradiction of Sir William's words in the letter they were not shown – declared that it was simply 'for the satisfaction of the family'. This was not reason enough as far as the doctors were concerned and, to their no doubt mutual relief, they prepared to take their leave.

Although Mr Powell was present during this exchange and would clearly have welcomed any evidence of foul play rather than negligence on his part, he did not intervene. This is just one of the curious aspects of the behaviour of the main participants at this stage but perhaps, as seems to have been the case with Lady Boughton, he was deferring to Donellan, feeling it was not his place to correct the only surviving male member of the household.

While the visitors were enjoying a belated supper, Donellan took the chance to quietly remind Lady Boughton that they would expect to be recompensed for their trouble. Parsimonious as ever, she happened not to have any ready cash to hand, so he paid them from his own pocket: six guineas to each of the three medical men and two for the anonymous assistant. Lady Boughton thought this excessive but Rattray was to complain later that he and Wilmer's services had been equated with those of a 'country apothecary'.

Before they left, Donellan asked if they would be reporting back to Sir William and Rattray said that he hoped to do so the following day. Even so, next morning Donellan wrote once again to the baronet. If his first letter, giving news of the death was disingenuous, this latest missive was a masterclass in ambiguity.

> Dear Sir,
> Give me leave to express the heartfelt satisfaction I enjoyed in the receipt of your letter, as it gave Lady Boughton, my wife, and self an opportunity of instantly observing your advice in all respects; I sent for Dr Rattray and Dr Wilmer; they brought another gentleman with them; Mr Powell gave them the meeting, and upon receipt of your last letter I gave it to them to peruse and act as directed.
>
> The four gentlemen proceeded accordingly, and I am happy to inform you that they fully satisfied us, and I wish you to hear from them the state they found the body in, as it will be an additional satisfaction to me that you should hear the account from themselves.
>
> Sir Theodosius made a very free use of ointments and other things, to repel a large boil which he had in his groin. So he used to do at Eton, and Mr Jones's, he told me often. I repeatedly told him to consult Dr Rattray, or Mr Carr, but as you know Sir Theodosius, you will not wonder at his going his own way, which he would not be put out of. I cannot help thinking but that Mr Powell acted to the best of his judgement for Sir Theodosius in this and the last case, which was but a

short time finished before the latter appeared. Lady Boughton expressed her wishes to Sir Theodosius, that he would take proper advice to his complaints, but he treated hers as he did mine. She and my wife join in best respects, etc

5th Sept. 1780   John Donellan
To Sir William Wheler, Bart

Whatever Donellan's motive – whether to spare the family more distress, or something more sinister – the clear impression is that the autopsy had been carried out and that nothing untoward had been found. Whatever his reasons, the actual non-event would in any case be revealed soon enough, once the doctors had made their report. Yet another puzzling aspect of this episode is that before sending the note he read it aloud to Lady Boughton for her approval and she reacted angrily, saying that such a letter should not be sent; it was not worth the paper it was written on.

He overrode her though, the letter was despatched, and Sir William naturally concluded that his instructions had been complied with and no trace of poison had been found. But if Donellan thought the matter was now closed, he was in for a disappointment.

Early next morning, Samuel Bucknill, a young Rugby physician, arrived uninvited on the Hall's doorstep. Bucknill was ambitious, and he saw this as a chance to take a significant step in his quest to achieve fame far beyond the confines of a small Warwickshire town. His ambitions were akin to those of Tertius Lydgate, the doctor in George Eliot's *Middlemarch*, her fictional portrayal of nearby Coventry, who intended 'to do good small work for Middlemarch, and great work for the world.'

Bucknill understood that the family desired an autopsy to be performed and that his colleagues from Coventry had failed to do this. He, however, was more than happy to oblige. He had his surgical instruments with him, so if the body could just be carried into the garden he would at the very least remove the stomach for investigation.

But Donellan flatly rejected this proposal. Dr Rattray and Mr Wilmer had declined to open the body and it would be quite improper to go against the opinions of 'men so eminent in their profession.' Bucknill laughed heartily at this, saying that they were mere 'country practitioners' and performing the operation would be 'a posy' for him. Donellan though was adamant, and the young upstart was forced to retreat, tail between legs.

Once again, however, Donellan's satisfaction was short-lived, for Bucknill was not so easily deterred and straightaway headed for Leamington to apprise Sir William of this latest turn of events. The baronet immediately fired off yet another letter and this time, despite the customary platitudes, he made no attempt to hide his anger.

> Dear Sir,
> From the letter I received from you yesterday morning, I concluded that the body of the late Sir Theodosius Boughton had been opened, and that I should receive an account from the faculty of the state that they found it in. I have not yet heard from them, but find that they found the body in so putrid a state that they thought it not safe to open it.
> I likewise find, that a young man of Rugby (Mr Bucknill) did attend, and offer to open the body, but it was not done. If Bucknill and Snow will do it, I by all means recommend it to you to let it be done, as it must be a satisfaction to you as well as myself, to have the cause of his sudden death cleared up to the world. If there is any danger in opening the body, it is to themselves, and not to the family, as the body may be taken into the open air. If I am not misinformed, Mr Bucknill is, or was very desirous of opening the body. I am, with respects to Lady Boughton, Mrs Donellan, and yourself, your sincere and obliged humble servant,
> Lemington, Sept 6, 1780
> William Wheler
>
> If Snow is from home, I do not see any impropriety in Bucknill's doing it, if he is willing. I will send Snow to Bucknill, that if Bucknill should be gone to Lawford Hall, he may follow him.
> To John Donellan, Esq. Lawford Hall

Bernard Snow, whose practice was based in the nearby town of Southam, was Sir William's personal physician and by involving him he was clearly trying to ensure that there would be no more shilly-shallying; and with the afterthought, he was attempting to make assurance double sure by avoiding any repetition of Bucknill's first attempt. Even so, despite his exasperation and concern for his reputation in the county, the baronet was maintaining the hands off approach he had shown throughout his guardianship. He was of course still having to come to terms with the death of his infant grandchild, but even so his attitude seems extraordinarily lax.

Similarly, despite her angry reaction to Donellan's latest letter, which had reawakened all her suspicions, Lady Boughton continued to stand back and allow him to deal with the medical men and, indeed, press ahead with the arrangements for the funeral.

Donellan's own behaviour is also puzzling. On the one hand, he seems to have been determined to prevent an autopsy at all costs, failing to inform Wilmer and Rattray about the poison rumours and fobbing off Bucknill with a spurious excuse, whilst at the same time he was urging the baronet to be present. The initial decision to call off the autopsy was taken by the Coventry physicians alone, with Donellan waiting for them downstairs, and although his letter to Sir William was clearly calculated to give a false impression of the evening's proceedings, he had urged the doctors to convey their conclusions to him.

As soon as he learned that this had not happened he wrote to Rattray reminding him of his promise. (The physician had not done so because on the day after the abortive visit he fulfilled an engagement at Brookswell, where he stayed the night, and in any case he had not considered it essential that he should call on Sir William in person.)

Donellan's own explanation for his inconsistent, not to say irrational behaviour, was that he panicked. He knew full well that if there was any suspicion of foul play he would be the prime suspect, and he was deeply conscious of the fact that when, in the presence of Mr Powell, he read the letter from Sir William first mentioning the rumours his hands shook uncontrollably. But this, he claimed, was a recurring symptom of a nervous complaint he had suffered from since his time in India and which had, understandably, reasserted itself at this time of great stress.

Also, his apparent anxiety to prevent a second attempt to open the body could simply have been to save Lady Boughton and his wife from any further distress. Certainly, he pressed ahead with the arrangements for the funeral, which was now set for the very day that Sir William wrote with his peremptory demand that there should be no more delay. On receiving this latest letter, Donellan immediately replied, in tones that were also markedly cooler:

Dear Sir,
In answer to yours, which I this moment received, I now, as I did yesterday in my letter, refer you and any one that pleases, for the

particulars respecting the state Messrs Rattray, Wilmer, Powell, and another gentleman, found Sir Theodosius's body in; they, agreeable to your directions, were by themselves upon that business, and I was in hopes you had seen them since I wrote to you yesterday morning.

He goes on to inform Sir William that the time fixed for the burial was three o'clock that day, 'and if you please to order it to be postponed until the state of the body is made known to you by the people you ordered to come here, please to let me know it before.' All well and good – except that this letter was not written until 'a quarter before one o'clock' in the afternoon, and, either because Donellan deliberately delayed sending it, or Sir William was not at home when it arrived, he did not actually read it until that evening.

Bucknill duly arrived at the Hall in mid-afternoon. The estate carpenter, together with the long-suffering plumber, Crooke, were standing by to open the coffin yet again, even though over thirty tenants – some of whom were to act as pall-bearers – had assembled in the entrance hall, ready to move on to the church. However, Donellan told him that as all the mourners lived locally the funeral could easily be put off to another day. Bucknill though, more circumspect this time, felt that he ought to wait for Mr Snow so that they could conduct the autopsy together, and Donellan – again contravening Sir William's express wish – failed to inform him of the postscript to his latest letter.

If Donellan really was set on avoiding an autopsy, fate in the shape of a black comedy of errors played into his hands. Bucknill could not wait very long for he was anxious to attend a patient living two miles away who was seriously ill. In fact, he was about to depart when a horseman arrived to say that the patient was very near death, and he hurried off, saying that he would return as soon as possible, no later he hoped than an hour and a half.

He had gone no more than a mile when he became aware of someone pursuing him at full gallop and calling out that 'Mr Snow is come.' Bucknill replied that he would be back within the hour, but when he did so it was to find that Snow had left. The Southam man had, in his turn, grown impatient and Donellan, in the presence of the mourners, urged him to go ahead with the operation on his own.

But, like Bucknill, he declined, contenting himself with questioning the female servants who had sat up with the body and also the two workmen.

The latter gave a vivid account of the putrified state of the corpse, the plumber adding that every time he soldered and unsoldered the coffin – and he had done this four times now – he had to make it so hot that he could not touch it without burning himself.

Snow therefore took it upon himself to give instruction for the funeral to go ahead later that day and, having collected his six guineas, he took his leave, missing the return of a perspiring Bucknill by a matter of minutes. He too departed, in high dudgeon, leaving Donellan to supervise the final arrangements for the funeral. The family crypt in Newbold church was opened and at seven o'clock that evening Sir Theodosius was at last laid to rest.

But if, as the paving slabs were replaced, Donellan heaved a private sigh of relief, disappointment awaited him. His troubles were only just beginning.

Chapter Seven

FAR FROM bringing closure, the funeral only intensified the gossip and speculation and it became clear that the only hope of silencing the clamour was for the twice aborted autopsy to be finally carried out and for this to be followed by an inquest into the circumstances surrounding the death.

The Rugby area was under the jurisdiction of the coroner for Coventry, Robert Fox, and on the morning of Saturday September 9th he along with eighteen hastily assembled jurymen entered the crypt of Newbold church to witness the exhumation of the body that had been laid there just three days earlier. The autopsy itself was to be carried out in the churchyard for the crypt could not accommodate all the interested parties.

As well as the coroner and his jury there were the five medical men involved in the two previous attempts, the Revd Parker, Donellan and Lady Boughton (Sir William Wheler was even now distancing himself from the proceedings) not to speak of the five hundred locals, crammed among the gravestones, and who would not have taken kindly to being deprived of their morning's entertainment.

Another factor, of course, was that the body was likely to be in an even more advanced state of putrefaction which, in the confines of the crypt, would be well nigh intolerable.

However, with the body placed on the Onely tomb, Drs Wilmer and Rattray could see that the features were much as they had been four days previously – swollen and blackened (but with no sign of the maggot). Now though, with the shroud removed, they saw that the discolouring went as far as the breast and dark spots covered the entire body, including the scrotum and penis.

After his abrupt exit and return, Mr Bucknill steeled himself to proceed with the dissection. The heart seemed to be in its natural state but the lungs were suffused with blood, the surfaces a deep red, almost purple, and with black specks.

The diaphragm was similarly discoloured while the kidneys and liver were, in Rattray's words, 'black as tinder'.

An incision of the stomach – which seemed to the watching physicians to be unnaturally inflamed – released about a spoonful and a half of slimy, reddish liquid, some of which Bucknill caught in a small phial. Edging forward, Rattray rubbed it between his finger and thumb but could not detect any 'gritty substance' in it.

In attempting to remove the stomach, Bucknill, the self-proclaimed master surgeon, accidentally cut through the bowels, releasing their contents. Even in the open air, the ensuing stench was so offensive that any more detailed examination was hastily abandoned. The corpse was replaced in its coffin and returned to the crypt, whilst the coroner, jury and witnesses moved on to the nearby house of the Parish Clerk, John Parker, for the opening of the inquest.

The fact that foul play was already the general assumption, with Donellan identified as the guilty party, was underlined by the fact that, just as in a full trial the accused could not testify on his own behalf, he was not one of those to be called to give evidence. Furthermore, the coroner took him on one side and suggested that he might prefer not to be present while the other witnesses gave their testimony but he rejected this presumably well-meaning offer.

The first to be called was Thomas Hewitt, aged twenty-three, a miller from Rugby. He stated that two months previously he purchased an ounce of occuli indicus berries from Mr Bucknill, together with a small quantity of spirits of wine. He boiled the berries in water, mixed with the wine, put this into a small bottle and delivered it to Sir Theodosius at the Hall. The young man thanked him and put the phial into his pocket – just as he did with that final dose brought to him by Samuel Frost. Occuli would seem to be a mishearing, either by the witness or the clerk recording his evidence, for cocculus is the berry of a fruit originating in India, and cocculus indicus was an ointment commonly diluted with alcohol to act as a narcotic and for the treatment of scabs or itching. This was presumably one of the means by which Sir Theodosius was 'quacking himself'. It was about this time that Mr Powell's services were first employed and the evidence would seem to undermine the apothecary's contention that his patient was generally in good health, and strengthen Donellan's contention that Sir Theodosius was showing symptoms of his recurring illness for some months before his death.

Lady Boughton was the next to give evidence, describing how on the morning of her son's death she poured the potion into a basin, leaving 'a large quantity of powder or sediment at the bottom of the phial,' then gave it to him. It had, she added, 'a very offensive and nauseous smell' but no mention was made of its resemblance to that of bitter almonds. On the crucial matter of Donellan's behaviour, she stated simply that when she showed him the bottle that had contained the mixture he added water to it then poured the contents into a bowl, dipped in his finger and declared that it had a nauseous taste.

Although this largely corroborates his own version of the incident, Donellan still reacted sharply when she reached this stage of her evidence, a fact that did not go unobserved by at least one member of the jury. 'When Lady Boughton said Captain Donellan rinsed the bottles,' William Crofts was to say later, 'I saw Captain Donellan catch her by the gown and give her a twitch.' Crofts was recalling the episode some six months later and his memory was a little awry: in this, her first narration, Lady Boughton did not use the potent term 'rinsed' and Donellan handled just one bottle, not the two or more of her later versions.

Donellan himself contended that the incident occurred several minutes previously when she was describing how she asked her daughter's maid if she knew where he was. She was, he said, speaking in such a low tone that he misheard, thinking that she said 'her daughter' and as Theodosia was not even up at that time he tugged at her sleeve and whispered a correction.

Even so, he was acutely aware of the potentially damning nature of Lady Boughton's evidence, and that evening he was still simmering over it, declaring to Theodosia, in her mother's hearing, that she had no business mentioning his washing the phial. She should, he told her angrily, confine herself to questions that were put to her, and that question had not been asked.

Thomas Powell, described in his deposition as 'surgeon', followed Lady Boughton and confined his evidence to a listing of the ingredients he had put together for the final draught, with instructions that it be taken the next morning. It was, he insisted, 'a medicine frequently given by the faculty and which the deceased had before taken without any inconvenience arising therefrom'. This was on just one occasion, he might have added but did not, the ingredients having been changed from the previous prescription, which had had an adverse effect on his patient.

Next came Sarah Steane, a widow from Long Lawford, who had been sent for to lay out Sir Theodosius. In her brief testimony, verified with an X for she was illiterate, she said that on the third day after his death she assisted in putting the body into the coffin and 'he seemed and appeared in every respect the same as any other corpse.'

William Frost, the coachman, followed her and declared that the baronet was, as far as he could tell, in a state of good health on the evening before his death. This led naturally to the rest of the medical evidence, with Bradford Wilmer and David Rattray being the first to be called, perhaps because as Coventry men they would have been known to the coroner.

Wilmer was quite frank about the limitations of his evidence. When he was first called to the Hall to examine the corpse, 'he found it in such a putrid state that opening the body, in his opinion, could not at that distance in time from the death of the deceased, determine the cause of death.' Mr Powell's mixture could not have brought it about but 'he is induced to believe that at this time it is impossible to tell what occasioned the deceased's death.'

Dr Rattray agreed that on their first visit he 'conceived nothing conclusive could be acquired from the dissection of the body, being so putrified', but on the second point he was prepared to go further than his colleague. Powell's concoction was harmless so whatever it was that Lady Boughton gave her son 'was probably the cause of his death.'

Although it was far too soon after that morning's events to give anything but a preliminary conclusion, both men described the main features of the internal organs and Mr Snow in his turn confirmed their evidence. Mr Bucknill had of course actually carried out the autopsy but he was the last to be called and could not add anything of value, beyond agreeing with Rattray that the potion given by Lady Boughton, whatever it contained – though neither of them was prepared to venture an opinion on this – was 'the probable cause of his death'.

Young Samuel Frost was next and he declared that when he saw his master in his bedroom on the actual morning of his death he was 'in his usual state of health and in perfect good spirits.' Apart from giving him his orders regarding the fishing net, Sir Theodosius said that he would shortly be sending him to Leicestershire on a matter of business for him.

It was five o'clock by now, but with virtually all the witnesses called and the jury thinking that all that remained was for them to consider their verdict – a task that could surely be despatched with the minimum delay – the coroner abruptly announced that the proceedings were adjourned. He gave no explanation for this, merely instructing the eighteen disgruntled jurymen to present themselves again at three in the afternoon the following day.

It is difficult to see why he did this. Full-scale trials, involving numerous witnesses, which today could last weeks or months were habitually completed within a day, and with emotions in the district threatening to get out of control, it would have seemed wise to complete the proceedings as quickly as possible.

Mr Fox will have known full well that only one verdict would silence the clamour, and it is possible that the admissions by the medical men that no definite conclusions could be drawn as to the cause of death made him reluctant to hand matters over to the jury. Certainly, at least according to Donellan, as people were dispersing, the coroner had a quiet – and one would have thought ill-advised – word with him, assuring him that as far as the inquest was concerned he had nothing to fear.

There was a further matter preoccupying Mr Fox: he was concerned about who would be paying for the inquest – in particular, although it was too delicate to actually mention, his fee. As the inquest had been called at the request of the family – or at least by Sir William Wheler acting on their behalf – would they be bearing the cost or should it be charged to the county? Donellan, relishing his role as head of the former, grandly replied that it would be disgraceful for the county to suffer any expense. If Mr Fox would let him know the figure, he would recompense him there and then. The coroner though had not yet made the calculations but would call at the Hall on his way back to Coventry and inform him.

Donellan therefore returned home feeling much easier in his mind and about four hours later Fox, accompanied by Mr Wilmer, arrived and were shown into the great parlour where they were met by their host together with Lady Boughton and Theodosia. However, when Donellan raised the matter of the costs the coroner said that he was still not able to name a figure as the proceedings were not complete. Even though their testimony, given under oath, had been read back to them and signed as a correct record, several of the witnesses would have to be recalled for further examination. Among these, he was sorry to say, was Lady Boughton.

Despite his unease at this development, Donellan insisted on giving him seven guineas on account, and he also paid Wilmer five guineas 'for his great trouble and the disagreeable business' (presumably the exhumation and autopsy) 'he went through.' Wilmer, solicitous for his colleagues' welfare, said that unfortunately they could not be present as they had patients to visit in the neighbourhood and Donellan, taking the hint, gave him a further five guineas apiece.

Everything therefore was set for a resumption the next afternoon but, with the jury dutifully assembled, their annoyance was increased tenfold when a message arrived to say that Mr Fox could not after all attend that day and the inquest would now be resumed on the following Thursday. Once again, no explanation was ever offered for this extraordinary decision but it only served to fuel still further the rumours and speculation. If the coroner's words of reassurance to Donellan were premature, his visit to the Hall and the fact that money had changed hands was even more unwise, and scurrilous talk began to spread of illicit influence being brought into play.

The comments by the anonymous author of *The Life of Capt John Donnellan* are typical of the common reaction: 'Unless we can suppose this gentleman to have been confused by the novelty of the business, or by his delicacy for the honour of a respectable family, it will be difficult to account for his behaviour on any grounds favourable to his reputation; but as his conduct, should the reports spread concerning it be founded in truth, will be probably noticed by the Court of King's-Bench, we shall forbear to enlarge any further upon it.'

Donellan though was left to wonder if the pressure was coming from another direction entirely. If Fox was right and the testimony given so far was insufficient to lay the blame squarely on the prime suspect, certain powerful individuals who were convinced of his guilt just might have been tempted to bring their weight to bear on the coroner.

Clearly fearful of the way the wind was blowing, and perhaps mindful of his involuntary reaction to Lady Boughton's testimony, he decided to remain at the Hall during the resumed hearing. He was in any case still not going to be given an opportunity to defend himself in person, so early on the Thursday morning he composed a letter addressed to the coroner and jury.

> Gentlemen,
> My understanding from report that you are to meet again today, I hold it my duty to give you every information I can recollect respecting the business you are upon, exclusive of what appeared before you last Saturday, when Lady Boughton and self were with you.
>
> During the time Sir Theodosius was here, great part of it was spent in procuring things to kill rats, with which this house swarms remarkably. He used to have arsenic by the pound weight at a time, and laid the same in and about the house in various places and in many forms. We often expostulated with him about the extreme careless manner in which he acted, respecting himself and the family in general; his answer to us was that the men servants knew where he had laid the

arsenic and for us we had no business with it. At table we have not knowingly eaten anything for months past which we perceived him to touch, as we well knew his extreme inattention to the bad effects of the various things he frequently used to send for, for the above purposes, as well as for making up horse medicines.

He used to make up vast quantities of golard, from a receipt which he had from Mrs Newsam; she will give you a copy of it if you please and it will speak for itself. Since Sir Theodosius's death the gardener collected several fish which Sir Theodosius laid – he used to split them and rub the stuff upon them. The gardener was ordered to bury the fish. The present men servants and the former ones for about two years back with William Matthews the house carpenter can relate the particulars respecting the above having been Sir Theodosius's common practice when he was able, or that he was afishing or attending his rabbits or at carpenter's work. Lady Boughton, my wife, and self have shewed the utmost willingness to satisfy the public respecting Sir Theodosius's death, by every act within the limits of our power; the accompanied letter from Sir William Wheler will testify the same, as well as our orders, that every one that came to the house should see the corpse before it was put into the coffin the 4th day, and the 8th day the corpse was sent to the vault at Newbold,

I am, gentlemen, your most obedient humble servant,

Lawford, September 14, 1780   John Donellan

Sir William's letter was presumably the one dated 4th September, where he expresses his satisfaction that the family are happy for the autopsy to be carried out but Donellan of course skates over the subsequent difficulties and in any case refers simply to the body being seen. The main thrust of his letter though is to tackle head-on the increasingly insistent speculation that the young man had been poisoned.

Golard or goulard water was used as a lotion to treat cases of inflammation of the joints in horses and cattle but was also a supposed cure for scabs and itching. (Thirty years later Samuel Taylor Coleridge tried 'to check the intolerable itching with a weak mixture of goulard and rosewater.') So this could well have been yet another of the self-administered remedies that Sir Theodosius was experimenting with.

However, it was derived from a sub-acetate of lead and was therefore highly toxic if swallowed by rats – or human beings. Also, although it was of course not known at that time, lead poisoning can be assimilated into the body through physical contact – as many individuals who had, in previous years, favoured the fashion for cosmetics made from white lead had found to their cost – and by his frequent handling of it, even in diluted form, he could have been adding unwittingly to his state of ill-health.

Amongst the swirling rumours surrounding the case, arsenic had become the increasingly favoured cause of Sir Theodosius's death, and the letter is clearly aiming to show that its presence was well-known to all the inhabitants of the Hall. However, the fact that it was so readily available could just as easily be seen as further evidence of Donellan's own guilt.

His fears about the adjournment seemed to be confirmed when, on the Thursday morning, the inquest was finally resumed – this time in the Assembly Room of the Bear and Ragged Staff tavern in Rugby, the very room where he had extricated his brother-in-law from several of his quarrels with local worthies. Before the proceedings got under way, Lord Denbeigh, who was keeping a watching brief on behalf of his friend, Sir William Wheler, had a private meeting in an adjoining room with Lady Boughton. Whatever was said during their half hour conversation, when she was recalled her testimony, particularly regarding the incident of the washing of the bottles, was considerably strengthened – and all to the detriment of Donellan.

This time, she claimed that when she indicated the fatal phial he 'swilled the bottle out with water and threw the water and the medicine which was left at the bottom of the bottle upon the ground.' When she expressed surprise at this, he said it was in order to taste it but he did not in fact do so. Instead, he took a second phial from the mantel-piece and threw away its contents in a similar manner. He then ordered her maid, Sarah Blundell, to remove both bottles and, despite her objections, he insisted and 'she believed they were removed accordingly.' She had also, she declared, heard Donellan advise her son to keep his medicines in his 'first room, and not in an inner room, which he kept locked, whereas any part of the family might have access to the former.'

She went on to describe Donellan's angry reaction to her previous evidence then, just in case the significance of her revised account had escaped the jury, she declared that 'the circumstance of the said John Donellan swilling the bottle led her to suppose that some unfair dealings had been carried on respecting her son, and that he had died by the medicine she had given him.' She concluded her evidence with the entirely gratuitous but damning observation 'that she was herself so much alarmed at it that she herself should like to be opened when she died.'

Sarah Blundell followed her mistress and duly confirmed the revised account of her clearing the room, adding that Donellan assisted her in this. She was the only other witness and her brief testimony would barely have lengthened the earlier hearing. The fact that although they had had four extra days to consider the findings of the autopsy, none of the medical men was recalled, increases the suspicion that the need for Lady Boughton to embellish her evidence was the sole object of the adjournment.

Certainly, with the testimony of the grieving mother still resonating, the jury could come to only one verdict and, after the minimum delay, this they duly delivered: that Sir Theodosius Boughton had been unlawfully killed and the perpetrator of this heinous crime was Captain John Donellan.

Two constables were despatched to Lawford Hall to effect the arrest and Donellan was forced to walk the two miles to Rugby, where the indictment would be formally delivered. News spread rapidly and the road was lined with jeering onlookers, including boys from Rugby School, skipping classes to witness the downfall of the hated individual who had imposed the iniquitous fishing ban.

As they neared town, his humiliation was complete when Taffy White, a half-witted youth who was usually the butt of local ridicule, appeared ahead of him dancing and grimacing, and exclaiming, 'Who's Taffy now? Who's Taffy now?'

Once in the Assembly Room, the coroner formally administered the indictment. (It is not recorded whether Mr Fox took the opportunity to raise the matter of his fee for the completion of the proceedings.) The indictment itself set out in detail the means by which Donellan allegedly brought about his victim's death, declaring that 'not having the fear of God before his eyes, but being moved and seduced by the instigation of the Devil, did feloniously, and of his malice aforethought, devising and intending Sir Theodosius Edward Allesley Boughton, Baronet, to poison, kill and murder, on the 29th day of August in the 20th year of the Reign of our Sovereign Lord George the Third, by the grace of God, of Great Britain, France, and Ireland, defender of the faith, with force of arms … a certain quantity, to wit, two drachms of arsenic, being a deadly poison … did put, infuse in, and mix together with water (the said John Donellan, then and there well knowing the said arsenic to be a deadly poison) … into and in a certain glass phial bottle, of the value of one penny.'

Quite why it was necessary to give the cost of Mr Powell's phial is unclear, but the crucial identification of the poison reflects the homing in of local speculation onto arsenic as the killer's instrument. None of the physicians had offered such a definite view, and Donellan might now have regretted his lengthy reference to it in his letter.

The indictment went on to spell out in detail his supposed substitution of the arsenic for Powell's concoction and the victim's subsequent fatal mistake, before reaching the conventional but nonetheless chilling conclusion 'that the said John Donellan, him, the said Sir Theodosius Edward Allesley Boughton, in manner, and by the means aforesaid, feloniously, wilfully, and of his malice aforethought, did poison, kill, and murder, against the peace of our said Lord the King, his crown and dignity.'

From there, Donellan was taken by coach to Coventry then on to Warwick to be clapped in irons and confined in the town gaol. He would be held there for over six months awaiting the next Assize, which was not scheduled until the following March. For the entire journey he was hemmed in by crowds, catcalling and gesticulating for all the world as though he was already on the way to his final destination – the scaffold.

Chapter Eight

THE INQUEST verdict and Donellan's arrest unleashed the equivalent of what today would be a media frenzy. The public prints, both local and national, carried stories which paid scant regard for the laws of sub judice or libel. The Coroner's behaviour came under particular scrutiny. The *St James' Chronicle* of 3rd October was one of several to report in terms laden with innuendo his conversation with Donellan following the abrupt adjournment of the Inquest, and his subsequent visit to Lawford Hall, during which money changed hands. The fact that Dr Wilmer, whose testimony earlier that day had seemed to rule out any certainty of a murder verdict, had also received payment from Donellan exposed him to the same scurrilous treatment.

There is in reality – on this occasion at least – no reason to doubt Donellan's version of these events, especially in view of the fact that if the Coroner was subjected to any undue pressure it was from another source entirely. Despite being confined to his prison cell, Donellan was kept abreast of the press coverage during visits from his solicitors, Edward Inge and Thomas Webb, and on 9th October the *Coventry Mercury* contained a brief item that, if not actually written by Donellan, was clearly reflecting his viewpoint:

> The reports in the public prints of the circumstances attending the death of Sir Theodosius Boughton, and the proceedings of the Coroner's Inquest in consequence of it, having been so contradictory, so various and so inconsistent with each other, that the public would do well to suspend their judgment upon this occasion, until the approaching trial shall have furnished facts, upon which a decisive opinion may be founded. Could it even be imagined that any of these printed authentic reports were strictly true, their chief tendency would be to prejudice the

Country against a man, who is at present a prisoner in Warwick gaol, and shortly to be tried for his life. The insinuation that some of the witnesses were closeted with Captain Donellan, after having declared (as is stated in the *St James' Chronicle* of October 3) upon their oath that the Baronet was poisoned, is an idea, as improbable, as it is absurd, and which the sensible part of mankind will reject with the contempt it deserves.

Lady Boughton was of course present at the meeting at the Hall, and she felt it necessary to issue her own 'Declaration', which the *Mercury* printed the following day:

A certain account having been industriously circulated in the public papers, said to contain my deposition at the Coroner's Inquest, held at Newbold, concerning the late melancholy event in my family, I think it necessary to declare that the same is *not true*, and the charge accusing Mr. Wilmer, Surgeon of Coventry, with having been *closeted* at my house, a considerable time with Mr. Donellan, on Saturday, the 9th of September, is a most detestable falsehood.

In testimony thereof I have this day affixed my name.
Lawford Hall   Anna Boughton
October 10, 1780

Despite these attempts to silence the rumours, the speculation continued unabated and Donellan felt it increasingly necessary to fight his corner. He was though having to cope with one hand tied behind his back. He complained bitterly that ever since his imprisonment 'he has been ordered into close confinement and refused the comforts usually extended to prisoners of his condition… Whatever letters or papers are either sent to or from him are publicly inspected by the Jailer, and he is even deprived of the assistance of his Lawyers, but in the presence of the Jailer or Under Sheriff, who may if they think proper betray his whole defence to his adversaries.'

Even so, he had been spared the horrors of the Warwick Gaol 'Dungeon', where forty or more prisoners, many of them religious dissenters – 'Quakers, Anabaptists and other unorthodox folk' – were kept at any one time. This octagonal-sided 'black hole', located beneath the courthouse, was twenty-one feet in diameter and nineteen feet underground. There was just one small grating in the roof for light and ventilation and eight posts were positioned round a central cess pit, each with a metal ring through which a long chain was inserted and fixed to the shackles that each prisoner wore. The space was at times so confined that the only position they could adopt was to lie prone on their sides.

Donellan's complaints were made in a letter addressed to the Editor of the *Coventry Mercury* which was published on the 16th October. Although it was signed A Friend to Justice, there can be no doubt as to its authorship:

> Sir,
> As very illiberal means have been taken in the public papers to prejudice the Country against Captain Donellan, charged with the Murder of Sir Theodosius Boughton, and to deprive him of that candour and impartiality the known characteristic of an English Jury; it may not be improper to contradict such groundless assertions, intended to answer no better end than to depreciate the characters of a few individuals, and to bring the unfortunate prisoner to a public trial, with all the disadvantages attending an exasperated country and a predetermined Jury.

The letter goes on to defend once again the conduct of the Coroner and Mr Wilmer, with the additional denial of the reports that Donellan has subsequently visited them in Coventry – a manifest impossibility given his confinement in Warwick Gaol. Moving on to the findings of the Inquest, the writer declares that 'the Jury, who were composed of neighbouring farmers, irritated at the Captain for having persuaded Lady Boughton to raise her rents, could never have altered their predetermined opinion, and the Captain in all events must have fallen a sacrifice to their passions.'

Stung by this slur, the jury members then joined the fray. In a letter, dated 20th October and published in the *Mercury* on the 23rd, and signed by all eighteen jurymen, with the exception of R. Jarratt, who appended his mark, they denounced the charge that before the Inquest even opened they had made up their minds on a guilty verdict. 'Is not this,' they proclaimed, 'a most uncharitable, cruel and impious declaration; an attempt to take away the characters of men, who always bore much better characters than the supposed author of the assertion.' In particular, they angrily refuted the claimed reason for their supposed bias:

'We are said to be neighbouring farmers and the public are led to imagine that we are rack-rented tenants under Lady Boughton, and from thence our prejudice arises. Only one of us is a tenant, and he rents a small plot of ground, not an acre. The majority of us never had any connection either with Lady Boughton or J. Donellan.'

They in their turn went on to cast near-libellous aspersions on Robert Fox, who had so inconvenienced them:

'The Coroner, for reasons best known to himself, would not on Saturday receive our verdict, but dismissed us, saying he would stay no longer (yet could find time to stop at Lady Boughton's that evening), and promised to meet us again the next day, which was Sunday, but never came. Surely this was strange conduct; and here we will make *one* assertion, to let the public a little into the light of this wonderful conduct. If the Coroner was not closeted with J. Donellan, it is certain that he called him out, whilst we the Jury were sitting, and was there and in the garden with him a full quarter of an hour ...

'We assert that Mr Fox acknowledged before the Magistrates and the Jury, at the last meeting, that Mr Wilmer was, on the evening of the Saturday on which the inquest was taking, with Mr Fox, the Coroner, at Lady Boughton's, and in the company with Lady Boughton and J. Donellan – the public may draw inferences.'

Wilmer was not the only medical man to find himself under attack. On the same day that the jurors' letter appeared, several of the London prints carried a report that 'the gentlemen of the faculty at Coventry are very angry at Mr Bucknill, surgeon at Rugby, being called the *operating* surgeon; but he had a much better and more noble spirit than they had and performed that operation, which they durst not.' The sarcastic tone is maintained in the account of the exhumation at Newbold: 'at sight of the body the *operating* surgeon was suddenly deserted by his *noble spirit* and appeared so panic struck that he made a precipitate retreat from the churchyard and was lost more than half an hour; when he returned he refused to proceed, alleging that nobody could compel him to do it. He asked Dr Rattray whether he would attend him at Rugby, if he should get a putrid fever, and kept the jury waiting two hours before he could be prevailed upon to begin, and had it not been for the positive injunction of the coroner, and the interference of the other gentlemen (one of who threatened if Mr Bucknill any longer delayed to perform his promise, to send an express for Sir William Wheler) the body of the late Sir Theodosius Boughton would have remained to this day unopened.'

Whilst Robert Fox and Bradford Wilmer maintained a lofty silence in the face of the innuendoes aimed at them, Samuel Bucknill was not the man to take such an assault lying down, particularly as he assumed that its source was his fellow physicians, who were jealous of his superior skills. In any case, the writer had not quite finished:

> 'We hear that a certain operating surgeon intends shortly to begin a course of anatomical lectures at Rugby, for the benefit of the ignorant part of the profession. Who having been long in practice are supposed to be totally unacquainted with modern improvement. He will clearly demonstrate to them not only that he dare open dead bodies, but also that he performs the operation in a manner entirely new and peculiar to himself, by which he dextrously separates the constituent parts of the subject with his fingers, without the assistance of edged tools or the least hazard of laceration. This new method is much preferable to that of Dr Hunter and Mr Cruishank, from whom the operating surgeon is falsely charged with having acquired his knowledge, as it supersedes the necessity of the knife, and the danger of cutting the fingers is thereby entirely done away.'

Within a few days, the *Mercury* had published a response from a certain Crito, the writer adopting the name of the eponymous individual in Plato's *Dialogue* who visits Socrates in prison and engages him in a discussion of the true nature of justice and injustice.

The anonymous author assures the reader, not entirely convincingly, that far from the letter being written at the surgeon's request 'he is at present entirely ignorant of it, and so far from that, I am well convinced Mr Bucknill was himself determined to take no notice of those malicious aspersions, and in truth they scarce deserve notice.'

On the matter of his retreat from the churchyard 'some time ago, in an accidental conversation with Mr Bucknill, among other things, upon this subject, he told me that he went to a neighbour's house to get a glass of wine etc.' It is not clear what the 'etc' refers to, but 'Crito' challenges anyone to find it 'so very strange for a person, about to undertake such a *dangerous* operation … when the body must be supposed to be very putrid, having been dead ten days, or more, and also from the effects of the poison … to take something as well to refresh himself, as to prevent the disagreeable smell which must, certainly arise from the state the body was in.' Far from being dilatory, 'Mr Bucknill performed the operation with the greatest alacrity, and more than this, had it not been for the spirited exertions of that gentleman, the body would have remained unopened, and a most complicated scene of villainy have remained undiscovered.'

The writer dismisses the final paragraph as being 'too frivolous, and the wit too *poor* to merit the least observation. It evidently appears to have been dictated by envy, the most ungenerous of all passions. To me it appears a tacit acknowledgement of Mr Bucknill's superior abilities as a surgeon, and a dread of him as a rival.'

Whilst such battles were being waged, the gossip continued unabated. The speculation about the motives of Fox and Wilmer in visiting Donellan – and receiving payment – originated presumably from within the Hall for neither of them would be likely to welcome the story becoming widely known. Lady Boughton's letter shows her annoyance at its emergence, so the likely source is one of the servants, many of whom resented the usurping of the young master's position by an upstart interloper.

A story that soon gained widespread currency was that, on the very evening of the day that Sir Theodosius died, Donellan came out into the garden and greeted Francis Amos with the words, 'Now, gardener, you shall live at your ease; it shall not be as it was in Sir Theo's days. I wanted before to be master, but I have got master now, and shall be master.'

That this episode ever occurred is highly improbable. It is true that Donellan clearly revelled in his role as titular head of the house and it is just possible that these words were uttered in a state of euphoria at a dream becoming reality. But even so, they were extremely ill-advised, spelling out in the crudest terms the motive for his supposed crime. He generally adopted a far more lofty attitude towards the servants than is suggested here, and, with his military background, was also a much more exacting taskmaster than the frequently incapable Theodosius.

In any case, he will have known full well that he would not remain as 'master' of Lawford Hall for long. The heir to the title was a second cousin who traced his claim through the male line from the son of the second marriage of the fourth baronet, and the incumbent family would have to make way, moving perhaps to one of their smaller properties in Northamptonshire.

Not all the servants were so hostile to Donellan; generally speaking, the females, more susceptible perhaps to his charm than the men, were much more favourably inclined towards him. In early October, Theodosia paid her first – and only – visit to her husband. She brought with her their infant son, John, but although Donellan clearly doted on the child he was left with Theodosia's maid, Sukey Sparrow, in the kitchen of Mr Roe, the gaoler, whose quarters adjoined the prison.

By this time, Donellan was sharing a cell with John Darbyshire, who had been imprisoned for debt, and in order to give husband and wife some privacy in what must have been a distressing encounter for both of them, he also went through to the kitchen. Another of the rumours surrounding the affair was that Sukey had been overheard denouncing Donellan as a murderer, and he took the chance to ask her about this.

She hotly denied ever having said any such thing. She had, she declared 'been sent for several times by the Justices and threatened by them if she would not disclose what she said at the country fair, and that she told them she said nothing against Mr Donellan there, nor knew anything against him.' In fact, 'he was as innocent of the charge brought against him as the child she then had in her arms.'

When Donellan heard of this he suggested to Mr Webb that both Sukey and Darbyshire should be called to testify on his behalf but the solicitor advised against this. They could both, in his view, prove to be unreliable witnesses. He was particularly dubious about Darbyshire, who had been made bankrupt twice and was currently in debt to the tune of five hundred pounds. However, as Donellan was soon to discover, the prosecution would have no such doubts about the man's integrity.

As for Sukey, her forthright defence of Donellan provoked a prompt response from Lady Boughton, who informed her daughter that she was 'a thief and a bad girl' who should be dismissed. Theodosia did so, only for the maid to be taken into Lady Boughton's own service, where a close eye – and ear – could be kept on her.

1. *St Botolph's Church, Newbold-on-Avon; the weathervane was erected in the 1970's, in place of the one that Sir Theodosius attempted to climb.*

2. *The Onely grave in St Botolph's churchyard, on which the autopsy on Theodosius was performed.*

3. *Sir Francis Buller, Bart, by Mather Brown (1792).*

JUDGE THUMB.

or — *Patent Sticks for Family Correction: Warrantal Lawful!*

4. *Buller aka 'Judge Thumb' by James Gillray (1782).*

5. The Shire Hall and Court House, Northgate Street, Warwick.

6. Outer cell door of the County Gaol, Warwick, at the time of Donellan's imprisonment.

Chapter Nine

ALTHOUGH THEODOSIA made just the one visit throughout the six months of his confinement, Donellan wrote to her on at least two occasions, both letters expressing concern for her own well-being. The second later, headed 'Warwick, the 8th of December, 1780', states:

> 'I am now informed that Mr Harris's clerk is here, and hope by this time that you have removed under the friendly roof I last recommended to you, and no longer remain where you are likely to *undergo the fate of those, that have gone already by sudden means*, which providence will bring to light by-and-by. In my first letter to you, the 14th November last, I mentioned a removal. I had my reasons, which will appear in an honest light in March next, to the eternal confusion of an unnatural being.'

The letter was sent unsealed. Donellan later claimed that this was accidental, arising from his haste in completing it before the clerk left, but the latter declared that when he pointed this out to Donellan, he replied that he had deliberately left it open so that its contents could be made public. If this was so, he had badly miscalculated for at the trial the prosecution seized on it as further proof of his guilt. He had, they argued, abandoned his futile attempts to provide a natural explanation, such as a chill, for Theodosius's death and was now trying to pin the blame on the unlikely shoulders of Lady Boughton. By 'the fate of those that have gone already by sudden means', he is clearly referring to the death from apoplexy of Theodosius's father, with the clear implication that she – 'unnatural' wife and mother – had for whatever reason brought about both deaths.

This interpretation of the letter was reinforced by John Darbyshire, who claimed that during several conversations his cell-mate had agreed that Theodosius must have been poisoned and when he was asked who was responsible he replied cryptically that the blame 'must lie among themselves.' Either Lady Boughton, the apothecary, one of the servants, or even the young man himself could be the guilty party – or even a combination of all four.

Theodosia of course did not take Donellan's advice for by now she was as convinced as her mother of his guilt. His solicitors, on the other hand, were sure that he was innocent – that is until, with the Assize approaching, they discussed with him who best to appoint as his counsel. Donellan suggested Mr Dunning, one of the leading – and therefore most expensive – advocates of the day. But when this was put to Theodosia she balked at this, either because of her certainty of his guilt or her inheritance of her mother's frugal ways, favouring instead the less costly Mr Newnham.

When they reported back to Donellan, he exploded with anger, exclaiming, 'And who got it for her?' By this he could well have meant his maintaining the well-being of the property and also his renunciation of his lawful claim on her inheritance. But the lawyers took it to mean that Theodosia, as her brother's heir, had benefited enormously from his death, and from then on they lost all faith in their client's innocence.

With the trial looming, the medical men, all of whom had been summoned to appear, had also been active. On the basis of Lady Boughton's description of Theodosius's reaction to the fatal dose, together with the smell of bitter almonds both she and they had detected, they concluded that the cause of death was not, as had first been thought, arsenic but a distillation of the equally toxic laurel water.

This is in fact the liquid form of hydrogen cyanide which, as every devotee of crime fiction knows, has a strong aroma of bitter almonds and, when a sufficient amount is ingested, induces virtually instantaneous physical collapse, convulsions and heart failure. (The Roman Emperor Nero was reputed to have disposed of his enemies by contaminating their wells with laurel water.)

Accordingly, three of them – Dr Rattray, Mr Wilmer and Mr Snow – but not the egregious Bucknill – got together to conduct experiments on a series of animals. Firstly, whilst Rattray held open the mouth of a greyhound, Wilmer poured two fluid ounces of laurel water down its throat. Within thirty seconds it had dropped down dead. Next, in the absence of a willing human guinea pig but with Sir William Wheler, stirring himself at last to play a more active role, present, they gave about a pint and a half of laurel water to 'an aged mare'. Within two minutes she fell to the ground, rolling onto her back and kicking violently. She lay convulsed, her eyes rolling, rearing up her head in agony and gulping until, after fifteen minutes, she died.

Then, at Southam, Rattray and Snow conducted a similar test on another old horse but this time, after displaying the same symptoms, the unfortunate creature took half an hour to expire. The bodies of both horses were opened and in each case the lungs were inflamed and suffused with blood in much the same way as those of Theodosius.

Meanwhile Bucknill, ever the loner, had been following his own path. He gave some of the fluid that he had collected when it flowed from Theodosius's stomach to a dog, but although it was to make the animal sick it had no worse effect.

All this was of course grist to the Prosecution's mill. But there was little need to strengthen their case further for Donellan's cause was looking increasingly hopeless. And it was not only his own solicitors who had lost faith in him; his defence counsel and the judge himself, Mr Justice Buller, were also convinced of his guilt. They were making the round of the Midland Circuit together and had spent the week prior to the Warwick Assize in Leicester. On the Sunday they dined together at an inn in the city and a fellow diner – another lawyer, named Cradock – later reported that 'the general conversation was Donellan, and his guilt was asserted by all; the only doubt seemed to be that as Lady Boughton, the mother, was all but a fool, her evidence, which was necessary, might not be effective; but it was acknowledged that she had been privately examined at the judge's chambers in town, and they thought she might be produced.'

To make matters even worse, and as Donellan himself recognised, feelings were running so high against him locally, 'with all the disadvantages attending an exasperated country', that anything other than a guilty verdict was well-nigh inconceivable. Certainly, today the trial would have been transferred to a locality where passions were less inflamed.

Even so, Donellan remained confident that he would be acquitted, outwardly at least. Just two days before the Assizes were due to begin, he wrote to an individual whose name has been deleted from the only surviving copy but who was presumably an acquaintance from his London days:

Warwick Gaol, Saturday, March 24

Dear -,
I expected you down here yesterday as you promised, but not seeing you I have been very uneasy. Let nothing prevent you from setting off

immediately, if this letter reaches you in London, and pray bring – with you. The people here are as violent as ever: their cruelty to me is not to be accounted for, as I never injured a single person in the country since I first came into it. However, their malice will be of no avail. As soon as the trial is over, *I will open your eyes on the whole of the unhappy business*, and which will satisfy you on the particular manner you mentioned in your last. My best compliments wait on Mrs -; *let her know I expect to pay her my respects in St Martin's-lane on Sunday se'ennight.*

I am, most assuredly, yours,

John Donellan

Although he was presumably unaware of it – and would not have cared to have it pointed out to him – Judge Francis Buller and Donellan had much in common. They both came from distinguished families, with long records of public service. The Bullers were prominent in many aspects of west-country life, particularly Cornwall, although Francis was born in Crediton, Devon, in 1746. They each had one child that died young, in Buller's case his older son, Edward, who was to die in February 1782, aged sixteen. Both men had eloped with heiresses – Buller's bride, Susannah Yarde, was twenty-three when they married, just a few years older than Theodosia. But whereas Donellan was a forty-year old man of the world, Buller had only recently left Ottery St Mary Grammar School, where he lived in the house of the Revd John Coleridge, father of the poet, and was a mere stripling of seventeen!

The two families were both outraged at the elopements and Susannah's ward, her uncle John, immediately cut her out of his will. However, as with Lady Boughton, he eventually accepted the situation – especially as Buller's career blossomed – and reinstated her as his heir before his death in 1773.

Little is known of Buller's marriage but it is to be hoped that he did not put into practice one of his more notorious pronouncements: that a husband was entitled to chastise his wife provided that the rod he used was no thicker than his thumb. This provoked a savage caricature by James Gillray in which he is depicted as 'Judge Thumb', vending 'Patent Sticks for Family Correction: Warranted Lawful'. The 'judge' carries two bundles of sticks and proclaims, 'Who wants a cane for a nasty wife? Here's your family amusement for Winter evenings; who buys here?' In the background a man is beating his wife, who cries, 'Help! Murder!' whilst he responds, 'Murder hey? It's law, you bitch: it's not bigger than my Thumb!'

Buller was also known to be a 'hanging judge', with a reputation for leaping too hastily to conclusions that impaired his conduct of criminal cases in particular. On the other hand, he could be relied on to get through the business of the courts with admirable despatch. The legal historian P.C. Scarlett described how on one occasion, when he was the sole judge on the Northern Circuit, 'there were eighty-six causes to be tried at York, one of which was a boundary cause that lasted sixteen hours, thirty-six at Lancaster, and forty to fifty prisoners at each place; but Mr Justice Buller concluded the whole Circuit in three weeks.'

In Warwick he was clearly anxious to maintain this reputation, as is shown in his initial Charge to the 'Grand Jury', from whose ranks the 'petit' juries would be selected to hear the individual cases. Their first task would be to hear the indictments and decide if the Crown had made a valid case – or 'true bill' – for the trial proper to proceed.

Prompt on the Monday morning he addressed all nineteen jurors, including their Foreman, the Hon. William Hewitt:

'Gentlemen of the Jury,
I am extremely pleased at your meeting me so early this Session, as by your timely attendance I hope I shall be able to get through the business of the county in the course of the week; and I am more satisfied at this circumstance as I perceive your calendar extremely loaded indeed, and that it actually contains a longer and heavier list of crimes than I have found charged in the Calendars of seven counties.'

The schedule included at least three cases of murder, but Donellan's was by far the most eagerly anticipated, and with a feeling for the courtroom as theatre, it would form the climax of the week's proceedings. But, with over twenty witnesses scheduled to appear in this trial alone, even Buller's skill would be tested. Therefore, he devoted most of his initial Charge to the case, singling it out as 'the first of consequence' in the entire list and trying to anticipate any likely stumbling blocks to a speedy conclusion.

One area that just might raise doubts in the jury's minds was that virtually all the evidence against Donellan was circumstantial. Where poisoning is suspected this is of course very often the case, for 'it is a crime,' the judge intoned, 'of so peculiar a nature that it is generally committed with the greatest secrecy, and over which the offender always makes use of every art and cunning to throw a veil. It is your duty, gentlemen, to throw off this veil and sift the business to the bottom. You are not to expect visible proofs in a work of darkness. You are to collect the truth from circumstances and little collateral facts, which taken singly afford no proof yet put together so tally with and confirm each other that they are as strong and convincing evidence as facts that appear in the broad face of day.'

The blatant bias and the broadest of hints that they would be presented with more than enough evidence, however circumstantial, to prove Donellan's guilt provoked considerable adverse comment from his fellow lawyers, many of whom disagreed with his view that such testimony was on a par with proven fact. Cradock declared that he was sorry to say that 'Judge Buller's charge at Warwick was imprudent, for it prejudged, or rather condemned, Donellan.'

The judge, though, did not leave it at that. He was keenly aware that doubts regarding the accused's guilt might be raised by the fact that he did not actually administer the fatal draught, and was in fact away from the house for much of the time that Theodosius was dying. Accordingly, he set out a hypothetical instance of such a killing by proxy, 'in which a man may be an hundred miles off and give poison to another to administer to a third. Here, the person who unfortunately administers the poison, if ignorant of the intention, is not guilty; but the person who gave it for that purpose, though at so great a distance, is guilty of murder.'

Hypothetical perhaps – and Donellan was only the short distance away at Newnham Wells when his supposed victim was in his death throes – but Buller's words were clearly aimed at strengthening still further the prosecution's case. In fact, the entire drift of the opening remarks was slanted towards the jury reaching only one possible verdict.

Under Buller's skilful management, by the Thursday evening, all the other cases had been concluded. He had imposed the death sentence three times, first on Thomas Hernes, a parish officer who had brought about by neglect the death of a pauper, Jonas Hutchinson, then two soldiers from Birmingham, John Hammond and Thomas Pitmore, found guilty of killing Wilfred Berwick, a butcher, in a bungled robbery.

So now everything was in place for the grand climax to the week, the case of Rex versus John Donellan, Esquire, for the wilful murder of Sir Theodosius Boughton, Baronet.

Chapter Ten

PROMPT AT seven o'clock on the morning of Friday, 30th March, Mr Justice Buller entered the Shire Hall in Warwick's historic Northgate Street. He wasted no time in admiring the entrance hall, even though there was much to admire in its elegant columns and ornate ceiling. He was also oblivious to the splendours of the courtroom itself, which was encircled by wrought-iron balustrading and eight Corinthian columns supporting an ornamental domed ceiling.

Instead, as he took his place looking down on the main body of the court, he merely satisfied himself that all was ready: the jury, grateful no doubt that the end of their arduous week was in sight; Mr John Webb, the Sheriff; the lawyers – five counsel for the Crown, together with their Instructing Solicitor (and the Boughton family's lawyer), Mr John Caldecott, from Rugby, and three counsel for the Defence, along with Mr Inge and Mr Webb; Mr Joseph Gurney and Mr William Blanchard, poised, with his personal blessing, to take down in shorthand every word of the day's proceedings, to be transcribed for their rival London publishers; alongside them the representatives of the public prints, both within the county and nationally – he noted the presence of the gentleman from the *Lloyds Evening Post*, who no doubt had his express carrier waiting to transport his verbatim account to Paternoster Row, to be printed and on sale by the following Monday at the latest; and finally the prisoner, Captain John Donellan, standing facing him in the dock, exuding a strangely calm not to say assured demeanour, despite the fact that from the hook placed immediately above the judge's chair hung the black cap that would be taken down and donned, should the need arise, to pronounce sentence of death.

Mr Digby, junior counsel for the Crown, read out the Indictment which, almost word for word followed that which had been drawn up in Rugby six months previously. It declared that 'John Donellan, late of the hamlet of Little Lawford, in the parish of Newbold upon Avon, in the county of Warwick, Esquire' did take 'a certain quantity, to wit two drachms of arsenic, being a deadly poison' infused and mixed it with water in a 'certain glass phial, the value of one penny ... did put and place in the stead of a certain medicine then lately before prescribed ... which the said Sir Theodosius Edward Allesley Boughton did take, drink and swallow down into his body, by means of which ... he then and there became sick, and distempered in his body and... did die.'

It is odd that, with the medical opinion now discarding arsenic in favour of laurel water as the poison, the Indictment was not reworded accordingly. The judge had noted this anomaly and in his Charge to the Grand Jury he had pre-empted any possible objection on the part of the Defence.

'If the Indictment should state,' he had declared, 'that the deceased died of any particular poison, and it should appear upon enquiry that he died of another poison, I am to inform you that the difference is immaterial, with respect to the law, it being held sufficient in such case that the deceased was poisoned.'

The allegation having been put to the accused and his plea of 'not guilty' duly recorded, the 'admired advocate' Mr Henry Howarth, KC (and Member of Parliament for Abingdon) then rose to open the case for the Prosecution. Despite the judge's desire for a speedy conclusion, his address to the jury set out in detail the basis of their case and lasted one and a quarter hours.

He began by returning to the problem that the judge had previously highlighted: 'The murderer by poison is not pointed out to justice by the bloody marks of his guilt, or the fatal instrument of his crime; his horrid purpose is planned in secret, is executed without his presence; his guilt can only be traced by circumstances, but circumstances sometimes do, and in this case I trust will as plainly reveal the guilty hand, as if an hundred witnesses testified the actual commission of the crime.'

After a few flattering words directed at Mr Justice Buller, 'a discerning judge, who will permit nothing to be placed in the scale of justice, but what ought to be weighed', he moved on to the motive for the crime. With Theodosius's death, his sister had inherited 'the greatest part' of his 'opulent fortune' and as she was married to the prisoner 'he, in her right, would have been entitled to a life estate in this considerable fortune.'

Donellan's claim that he had revoked this right in a legally binding document was ignored by both the Prosecution and the Defence, and Mr Newnham, leading for the latter, also saw no point in putting before the court the will that his client had drawn up shortly after his marriage in which he bequeathed to Theodosius any property he would inherit in the event of his wife's dying first and without issue.

Mr Justice Buller might or might not have been determined to be even-handed in his conduct of the trial, but the scales of justice at that time were heavily weighted against the accused. Not only did they have no chance to give evidence on their own behalf, beyond a brief, previously prepared, statement, but defending counsel did not have the luxury of addressing the jury, either at the beginning or the conclusion of a trial. All they could do was intervene on their clients' behalf, either during the prosecution's opening remarks or the examination of witnesses. There were in fact several assertions made by Mr Howarth in the course of his address that would not have withstood close scrutiny but Newnham, for whatever reason, let virtually all of them pass unchallenged.

Howarth was again skating on thin ice when he moved on to the events immediately surrounding Theodosius's death and tried to reinforce the impression that prior to this he was 'possessed of a good constitution, affected by no indisposition that could at all endanger his life.' He was, it was true, suffering from 'a slight venereal disorder' but this was being treated to good effect by Mr Powell.

He then described Theodosius's movements during his last afternoon and evening: the bringing of the final potion, his return from fishing 'in perfect health and good spirits', and his going to bed still 'apparently in good health'. In his narration of both this and the events on the fatal morning, he relied heavily on Lady Boughton's account. He went into considerable detail, fearful perhaps of how his key witness would perform, especially under cross-examination.

Having established in the jury's mind, he hoped, that the concoction that was given could not possibly have been the 'harmless draught' prescribed by Mr Powell, but was instead poison, namely a distillation of laurel water, he then went on to make what he saw as the vital point that 'the prisoner at the bar was skilled in distillation'. When, prior to the trial, he had learned that Donellan had his own personal still, he had exclaimed, 'Now I have the rope round his neck which will hang him!'

Certainly, both in his opening address and through witness testimony, he did his best to drive this home. Among those whose evidence the jury would shortly hear was the cook at Lawford Hall. She would tell them how, about two weeks after Theodosius's death, Donellan gave her his still filled with lime, which would of course have removed all trace of whatever had last been distilled in it, and ordered her to clean it out and dry it in the oven. Donellan told her that he had put the lime in the still then placed it under his bed in order to kill fleas, 'an excuse,' commented counsel witheringly, 'more ridiculous or more improbable it is not easy to suggest.'

Returning to the morning of Theodosius's death, he highlighted the affair of the washing of the phials. The accused, he said, took up each of the two bottles in turn, shook them, rinsed them then threw the contents 'into a bason of dirty water standing in the room.' There was no mention of this 'bason' at the Inquest, either by Lady Boughton or the maid, but as Howarth knew full well, this was the version of events she would shortly be giving to the court and, to fix it all the more firmly in the jury's mind, he anticipated it here, with of course no mention of the discrepancies in her Inquest testimony.

Newnham allowed all of this to go unchallenged, leaving his opposite number free to indulge in one of his more rhetorical flourishes. Referring to Donellan's supposed conduct, he demanded, 'How is this to be accounted for? What ingenuity can gloss over this transaction? How can it be reconciled to any idea of innocence?'

He then attempted to dispose of any other possible explanation for the death of 'this unfortunate young man', dismissing, for example, the idea that he had caught cold whilst fishing, or that the cause was 'the venereal disorder going through the family.' He did not elaborate on this last point and the Defence team did not pick up on it, either here or at any stage of the trial, but it would seem to be a clear indication that Theodosius's syphilis was indeed congenital, which would have accounted for both any temporary remission of the symptoms and their sudden return in even graver form – and, most important of all, could have formed the basis for a plausible alternative reason for his death.

Howarth then turned to the exchange of letters between Donellan and Sir William Wheler. Once again, he emphasised those elements that militated against the accused, for example his first letter's failure to describe the traumatic manner of Theodosius's death, but he either made scant reference to or omitted altogether the points in the prisoner's favour. Whilst mentioning Sir William's unwillingness to be present during the autopsy, he failed to show that this was despite Donellan's express wish for him to be there. Similarly, when dealing with the accused's letter of 5th September, describing the physicians' first visit to the Hall, he quoted his assertion that 'the four gentlemen proceeded accordingly, and I am happy to inform you that they fully satisfied us.'

'Good God!' exclaimed Howarth, not one to ignore the chance of another theatrical flourish. 'In what does this satisfaction consist? What opinion was formed? Not a single circumstance was ever mentioned; not a single enquiry ever made; not a single opinion ever expressed to the prisoner. Yet upon this he writes back to Sir William Wheler that *they have fully satisfied us.*'

Having taken Donellan's words out of context, and ignored the fact that the doctors had told him that in their view, because of the advanced state of putrefaction, there was no point in opening the body, Counsel informed the jury that he would not at that stage quote anything further from the letter as it was not 'material for your consideration.'

Not even Newnham could let this pass, and he finally intervened, requesting that the whole of the letter be read to the court. Howarth duly obliged, completing the sentence he had previously cited: 'I am happy to inform you that they fully satisfied us, and I wish you would hear from the state they found the body in, as it will be an additional satisfaction to me that you should hear the account from themselves.' But in a clear attempt to play down Donellan's injunction to the medical men to report directly to Sir William, he launched himself into another rhetorical display: 'Now what is to be heard? What information is to be gained by seeing these gentlemen, by hearing what they have to say? I will tell you the whole of their information. We saw the body, it appeared to us in a great state of putrefaction; we made no particular observation; we have formed no opinion; we can give you no light into the matter.'

Howarth then read out the remainder of the letter which, he declared, 'goes on very artfully to state, and to account for the death of Sir Theodosius from some illness he laboured under.' It was, he claimed, 'calculated still to mislead Sir William Wheler, is calculated to allay his suspicions, and to account for his death from other causes than poison.'

Having dealt briefly with the further abortive attempts to open the body by Bucknill and Snow, and the exhumation and autopsy, all of which he assured the court would be described in detail by witnesses, he turned to the incident at the Inquest when the accused caught Lady Boughton by the sleeve as she was describing the washing of the bottles. This, Howarth declared, 'is a circumstance that cannot be explained by any possibility. It cannot be imputed to folly; no art can explain it away', even though of course Donellan had offered the alternative explanation that he had misheard her and thought Lady Boughton had said that she had spoken to his wife, who was still in her room, rather than the maid.

Howarth then gave the court a foretaste of the testimony of John Darbyshire, Donellan's cell-mate whom, it will be recalled, Mr Inge had decided was too untrustworthy to be called as a witness. The Prosecution clearly had no such qualms and Howarth outlined a series of conversations that he would be claiming to have had with the accused, during which Donellan acknowledged that the cause of Theodosius's death was poison but sought to put the blame on anyone but himself.

Finally, by way of reinforcing Donellan's acceptance that the instrument was poison, he was about to read from a copy made by the bearer of the letter written to Theodosia urging her to remove herself from Lawford Hall. Before he could begin, however, Newnham made his second intervention, asking the judge to rule whether a copy of a letter could be used as evidence. But Mr Buller had no hesitation in allowing it, declaring, 'It depends upon the manner in which they lay it before the court; they must give the best evidence that the nature of the case admits. Now the custody of Mrs Donellan in point of law, is the custody of the prisoner.'

This failed totally to answer Newnham's objection but he did not press the point and Howarth was free to go ahead and read the letter, stressing the scarcely veiled imputation of Lady Boughton's guilt with its warning that if Theodosia remained at the Hall 'you are likely to *undergo the fate of those that have gone already by sudden means.*'

Given all the missed opportunities to challenge the opening address, Newnham's intervention here was seriously ill-judged for his reluctance to have the letter read merely stressed the threat it posed to his client and made it even less likely that the jury would swallow the line that Lady Boughton was the real killer. Certainly, it paved the way for Howarth's portentous peroration: 'Justice demands the punishment of the murderer; it remains only for your verdict to determine the guilt, and to consign the criminal to his fate.'

With these words ringing round the courtroom, Howarth resumed his seat and the first witness for the Prosecution, the apothecary, Thomas Powell, took the oath. Mr Wheeler, junior counsel for the Crown, had been deputed to lead him through his testimony. He began by asking about his view of Theodosius's health during the two months prior to his death, which the apothecary confirmed had occurred on the 30th August last.

Q. In what state of health was he when first you attended him?

A. He had got a venereal complaint upon him.

Q. To what degree?

A. Not very high, rather slight, a fresh complaint.

His use of the term 'fresh' was a further indication that the illness was a recurrence of a long-standing condition but the Defence once again failed to exploit this.

Powell then repeated the evidence he had given at the Inquest, listing the items he had prescribed: 'four doses, two of manna and salts, the other two of rhubarb and jalap' together with 'an embrocation to wash himself with.' He did not though offer any explanation for the change of ingredients after the first two doses until, under further questioning, he said that the first prescription had made his patient 'sick'.

The last draught was collected from him on the Tuesday by Samuel Frost. At Wheeler's prompting, he produced a two-ounce phial, the same size as the one he had sent and containing the same ingredients – rhubarb and jalap, spirits of lavender, nutmeg water and simple syrup. Following their obviously pre-rehearsed script, counsel continued:

Q. I see you have another draught in your hand?

A. Yes.

Q. What is that?

A. The same, except the simple water; there is the same quantity of rhubarb and jalap.

Q. What is added to that?

A. Laurel water.

So far so good. But at this crucial moment, with the introduction of the alleged murder instrument, Wheeler's failure to prepare his brief as thoroughly as he should have done, disrupted the harmonious rapport between himself and his witness. Returning to the first phial, he went on, 'You mentioned before that this was sent upon the Tuesday. It was, I think, upon the Thursday that Sir Theodosius Boughton died?'

Powell had already stated that his patient had died on the 30th, so it is scarcely surprising that he responded curtly, 'No. On Wednesday morning.'

'Was you then sent for to Lawford Hall?' enquired counsel and Powell, ensuring that he had got it right this time, replied, 'On the Wednesday morning I was.'

Q. Who was the person that came for you?

A. William Frost.

Q. The same man that you had before sent the draught by?

Powell, who had just three minutes earlier identified that individual, corrected him even more testily. 'No. His name was Samuel Frost.'

Shaken perhaps by these elementary errors, it was then the apothecary's turn to introduce some inadvertent comedy into the proceedings, with his counsel struggling to elicit a simple but vital statement of fact from him. Referring to

Powell's first view of his patient on that Wednesday morning, he enquired, 'In what situation did you find Sir Theodosius Boughton?'

'I saw no distortion' came the reply.

'What did you see?' persisted counsel, but all that the witness could offer was, 'Nothing particular.'

In desperation, Wheeler then asked bluntly, 'Was he alive or dead?' and at last he got the response he wanted: 'He had been dead near an hour.'

The apothecary's evidence ended with his account of a brief conversation with Donellan in which the latter seemed intent on persuading him that the young man had 'taken cold' and had actually died 'in convulsions.' In his brief cross-examination, Mr Newnham concentrated on this last point:

Q. You say that Mr Donellan told you that Sir Theodosius died of convulsions, and that was all the conversation about it?

A. Yes.

Q. Did it not occur to you, as a physical man, to enquire when these convulsions commenced, and when Sir Theodosius died?

A. The convulsions took place soon after the draught was taken.

Q. What idea have you of *soon*?

A. A quarter of an hour, or sooner.

Q. Do you know for certain?

A. I do not.

Q. Why did you not enquire?

A. I did enquire.

Q. You saw Lady Boughton?

A. Yes.

Q. Had you no conversation with her?

A. Yes. She said he was convulsed soon after he took the medicine.

Q. Did you not enquire how soon?

A. He was convulsed almost immediately.

By labouring this point, the Defence was presumably aiming to draw a link with the death 'of apoplexy' of Theodosius's father, with the suggestion that it was a sign of an inherited weakness. But this was not, at this stage, spelt out and the possible parallel would have been lost on the uninitiated.

Mr Howarth took over the questioning of the next witness, Lady Boughton, and he steered her skilfully through the potential shoals of her testimony, although not without some hiccups along the way. The first occurred early on when he came to the proposed visit of Mr Fonnereau and Theodosius's intended return with him to Northamptonshire. In his opening words to the jury, he had said that Theodosius planned to be away until his coming of age, thus giving added urgency to Donellan's murderous designs. But Lady Boughton was unable to confirm this:

Q. Had you heard from Mr Donellan anything respecting the stay that Sir Theodosius would probably make in Northamptonshire?

A. I don't recollect.

Q. Was his stay intended to be long or short?

A. My son said Mr Fonnereau was to stay with him a week, then my son was to return with him to Northamptonshire.

Q. Was he going to stay a long or short time there?

A. He did not say how long.

Similarly, Lady Boughton directly contradicted Howarth's assertion in his preamble that on Theodosius's final fishing expedition he was accompanied by all the Hall's menservants:

Q. After he had gone out a fishing what men servants were left behind in the family?

A. The gardener and the coachman, and John, the footman.

Q. Were there either of the men servants with Sir Theodosius a fishing?

A. Yes; Samuel Frost was the only one.

Rapidly changing tack again, counsel moved on to her version of the events of that last evening – her walking in the garden with her daughter, with no sight 'to the best of my remembrance' of Donellan until he joined them at seven o'clock, claiming he had 'been to see them a fishing, and that he would have persuaded Sir Theodosius to come in, lest he should take cold, but he could not.'

Howarth then guided her without mishap through the traumatic events of her son's death. Taking up the two phials that Powell had produced, he first gave her the one with the genuine draught, asked her to open it and smell it 'and inform the court whether that smells at all like the medicine Sir Theodosius took.'

'No,' she replied firmly, 'it does not.'

'Please to smell this,' continued counsel, handing her the bottle containing laurel water, and back came the response, 'This has a smell very like the smell of the medicine which I gave him.'

The next danger point though came with her description of the washing and removal of the phials. As Howarth was all too aware, her account would differ in crucial respects from the two versions she had offered at the Inquest. This time, instead of Donellan *either* confining himself to one bottle, adding water to it, pouring it out and tasting it, *or* dealing with the two phials, swilling out both and, with no attempt to taste either, throwing the contents on the floor, she said that after pouring water into the first bottle he 'shook it then emptied it out into some dirty water which was in a wash-hand basin.' Then, despite her remonstrances, 'he snatched up the other bottle and poured water into it and shook it, then he put his finger to it and tasted it.'

Even allowing for her understandably confused state of mind at this distressing time, her recollection is clearly at fault. Any one of the versions *might* have been accurate, but with them becoming increasingly incriminating as far as Donellan is concerned, it is just as likely that none of them is a true record of this vital episode.

The testimony moved on to the clearance of the room, done, Lady Boughton claimed, while her son was still alive. Anticipating perhaps the line likely to be taken by the Defence, Howarth elicited the admission that she was basing her allegations on assumption rather than established fact.

She declared that 'as soon as Sarah Blundell had put the clothes into the inner room, Mr Donellan, while my back was turned, put the bottles into her hand again and bid her take them down, and was angry she had not done it at first.'

Q. Did you see the bottles put into her hand the second time?

A. I did not.

Q. Did you hear any order given by him?

A. No; but Sarah Blundell told me so.

Conscious that her allegations were based solely on hearsay, the judge intervened.

Q. How soon did you perceive that the bottles were gone?

A. I did not observe it directly.

Q. But how soon did you find out that they had been removed?

A. I cannot tell the time.

Q. Before you left the room yourself, did you discover that the bottles were gone?

A. I did not.

None of this took the matter much further and Sarah Blundell could not be questioned because she was dead. After giving birth to her illegitimate child she had been instantly dismissed and, despite being mortally ill, sent away from the Hall on a farm wagon. But nothing of this shameful episode was revealed during the trial, and Mr Howarth gratefully took over the questioning again, swiftly leading his witness on to what must have seemed at first sight an even more damning incident.

Q. In the course of that morning, do you remember having said anything to Mr Donellan, or he to you, as to the suspicions entertained of the medicine he had taken?

A. Sometime afterwards I was down in the parlour; Mr Donellan and my daughter were there. Mr Donellan, in my presence, said to his wife that her mother (meaning me) had been pleased to take notice of his washing the bottles out, and that he did not know what he should have done if he had not thought of saying he put the water into it to put his finger to it to taste.

She had made no mention of this at the Inquest but it does of course closely resemble the story she told on her second appearance there of Donellan's reaction to her including the bottle washing episode in her evidence, and which she now went on to repeat. She has clearly either confused the time when this episode occurred or turned a single event into two separate incidents, with the crucial addition of Donellan's particularly unfortunate final turn of phrase.

Despite Mr Newnham's conviction of his client's guilt he owed it to him – and his own professional reputation – to mount at least a token defence, and, with the conclusion of the Crown's examination, Lady Boughton provided the easiest of targets.

In her evidence-in-chief she had echoed Mr Powell's contention that immediately before his death Theodosius had 'seemed very well', but Newnham reminded her that nearly four years previously she had been expressing concern about her son's health. He referred her to a letter she had written to Donellan and her daughter when they were living in Bath.

'Had not you,' he enquired, 'written to Bath in the year 1777 that his fine complexion was gone, and he was in a very bad way?'

'I said,' she replied, 'I was afraid he was in a bad way, for his complexion was altered.'

But Counsel was not going to let her escape with this sophistry, insisting, 'I quote your words, "his fine complexion was gone" ', and this elicited a reluctant, 'Yes.'

Newnham could have pressed home his advantage, asking why she had felt it necessary to remove Theodosius from Eton and place him under the care of Dr Kerr in Northampton. She had in fact enlisted the services of three medical practitioners during this time and, at Donellan's prompting, received notice to produce to the court 'all the bills she has paid to the different surgeons and apothecaries at any time employed by Sir Theodosius.' His Counsel, however, saw no point in asking for them, even though they would have reinforced the impression that the young man's health was much worse than had been claimed.

Instead, he moved on to Donellan's claim to have rescued Theodosius from various potentially fatal escapades, and Lady Boughton grudgingly confirmed his interventions to forestall duels being fought, on at least one occasion at her own instigation. She had little choice for she would have been aware that witnesses were present, waiting to confirm these episodes, but it was a different matter when it came to the incident of the weathercock, where with Theodosius dead there was no-one to corroborate Donellan's story:

Q. Do you recollect your son telling you that he went up at Newbold to the top of the church steeple, and that if it had not been for Mr Donellan, who caught him in his arms, he must have broke his neck?

A. He did not tell me that.

Q. Did not he tell you that he went up to the top of the church?

A. Yes. But he did not tell me about being in any danger.

Q. Did not your Ladyship, when he told you he had met with an accident, and an escape, enquire into the particulars of it?

A. I don't remember that he did tell me so.

Q. Do you remember no circumstance – don't you remember his mentioning that part of the church tumbling down when he was at the top of the church?

A. No.

Q. Did not you return home together in the coach – and did he not mention it in the coach to you that he had been at the top of the church, and had fallen in going up to the weathercock?

A. I don't remember any thing of it.

This was far from being her only attack of amnesia. When questioned by Mr Howarth about the events of the evening before Theodosius's death, Lady Boughton had qualified her assertion that she had seen nothing of the accused for several hours after the early afternoon dinner as being 'to the best of my recollection.' She presumably hoped that the proviso would provide adequate cover for any shortcomings in her account, which was of course totally at odds with Donellan's version.

At his urging, Dand and Matthews, the two workmen whom he claimed they had both conversed with, were present at the court and ready to testify but

Newnham decided against calling them, on the grounds that they could only account for his movements for part of the day and not provide a complete alibi. Even so, if they had confirmed his story, Lady Boughton's bias against him would have been thrown into sharp relief and her credibility seriously compromised.

Although she was no doubt relieved to escape from this particular exchange unscathed, as the cross-examination continued her lapses of memory became increasingly frequent. Her account of the conversation in the parlour shortly after her son's death posed a particular danger for the Defence, and Counsel set about dismantling it:

Q. Did your Ladyship ever mention, when examined before the Coroner, this fact, that Mr Donellan said, "I should not have known what I should have done, if I had not thought of saying that I did it to put my finger in to taste"?'

A. I did mention this before the Coroner. My evidence was, he said, that I told him of his washing it. I asked him why he did so. He said, he did it to put his finger to it to taste.

But this blatant prevarication could not go unchallenged.

Q. I asked your Ladyship whether you disclosed before the Coroner that Mr Donellan told Mrs Donellan, in your hearing, that if he had not thought of saying that he did it to put his finger in to taste, he should not have known what to have done. Did you mention that circumstance before to the Coroner?

A. Yes.

Q. And swear it?

A. Yes.

Q. I believe you was examined a second time. Was it upon the first or second examination?

A. I am not certain.

Q. Was your examination read over to you before you signed it?

A. Yes.

Q. I wish to ask your Ladyship again whether this circumstance was disclosed in your evidence?

A. I said he told me that he did it to taste.

Q. Your examination was read. There is no such thing as that contained in it.

With the witness growing increasingly flustered, Newnham moved on without pause to another of her assertions:

Q. Did you mention the circumstance of the coachman being sent for into the parlour, and Mr Donellan's asking him if he did not remember his going out at the iron gates at seven o'clock in the morning; and upon the servant's answering in the affirmative, Mr Donellan saying, "Will, now you are my evidence"? Was that mentioned by your Ladyship before the Coroner?

A. I mentioned it to Mr Caldecott. But whether I mentioned it before the Coroner, I cannot remember.

Approaching the end of his cross-examination, Counsel turned to the matter of Theodosius's possession of considerable amounts of poison. Having elicited the admission that she was aware of her son's amusing himself by laying poison for fish, he went on:

Q. Where was it he put those things that he used to amuse himself with? I won't mince the matter. Don't you know of his buying large quantities of arsenic?

A. He sent for a pound. And after he was dead, a quantity of arsenic was found in his closet.

Q. Where did he use to keep that?

A. In his inner closet.

Q. Which was sometimes locked.

A. Mostly.

Newnham was clearly preparing the ground for an alternative explanation for Theodosius's death, quite possibly at his own hands, and Howarth, sensing the danger, rose to re-examine his witness. He tried to divert attention away from the poison by countering the impression created by Donellan's apparent concern for his brother-in-law's well-being.

Q. You have been asked of instances of friendship shown by Mr Donellan to your son. What was Mr Donellan's general behaviour for some months before he died? Did he treat Sir Theodosius with respect, friendship and tenderness, or otherwise?

A. About a fortnight before my son's death, I heard –

The judge, fearing perhaps that she was about to embark on another excursion into hearsay, interrupted her:

Q. Have you heard your son say any thing about Mr Donellan's behaviour at the time when he gave the relation mentioned by Mr Newnham?

A. They used to have words, to be angry with each other. They did not in general live in friendship or intimacy.

With his brief moment of ascendancy slipping away, Newnham took up the questioning again, attempting to put this in a more innocuous light:

Q. It was your Ladyship's house?

A. Yes.

Q. I presume they had those sort of words that occasionally happen in families, more or less?

A. I paid no great attention to it.

Finally, with the witness now facing questions from three directions at once, the judge brought her back to the supposed incident in the parlour:

Q. After you got into the parlour, was there any conversation between you and the prisoner, previously to his saying you had been pleased to take notice of his washing the bottles?

But this simple question evoked yet another failure of memory:

A. I do not recollect any, but he was talking to Mrs Donellan.

Q. Was that spoken in any passion or resentment, or how?

This time, with the appropriate response virtually dictated to her, there was no problem with a reply:

A. Rather in a way of resentment.

And on this note, far less favourable to the accused than had been the case just minutes earlier, Lady Boughton's ordeal by testimony came to a merciful close.

Chapter Eleven

CATHARINE AMOS, the Lawford Hall cook, followed her mistress on the witness stand and, as befitted her lowly status, she was questioned by Mr Geast, Junior Counsel for the Crown. She, along with Sarah Blundell, had been summoned to Theodosius's deathbed and she gave a vivid account of his final moments:

Q. When you came into the room in what situation was Sir Theodosius Boughton?

A. He did not stir hand or foot, but frothed at his mouth. I wiped the froth four or five times from his mouth.

Q. Was the body motionless?

A. The stomach heaved very much.

Q. Was there any noise?

A. He guggled at the throat.

She could not throw any light on the bottle washing as she had left the room by then because, as she put it, 'my work lay below stairs.' She did though meet the accused in a corridor shortly afterwards and he told her that 'Sir Theodosius was out very late over night a fishing, that it was very silly of him as he had been taking such physic as he had been taking of, before (that) time.' However, on the day that the body was finally opened, she saw him again and this time he offered another explanation. 'He said there was nothing the matter, that it was a blood vessel had broke which had occasioned Sir Theodosius's death.'

Counsel then moved on to one of the most damning episodes, in the Prosecution's eyes at least, in their entire case:

Q. You said you was cook maid?

A. Yes.

Q. Was the oven under your direction?

A. Yes.

Q. Was anything brought to you at any time?

A. Yes, a still.

Q. Who brought it?

A. Mr Donellan.

Q. When was it?

A. Some time after Sir Theodosius's death.

Q. How long after?

A. To the best of my remembrance it might be a fortnight.

Q. What was there in it?

A. Nothing. It had been washed. He desired me to put it into the oven to dry it, that it might not rust.

Mr Geast saw no point in labouring this further, trusting that the jury would draw the inevitable conclusion, and the Defence made no attempt to counter any of her statements, despite the fact that Donellan had furnished them with at least one argument in his favour. He claimed that he had only put lime into the lower section of the still and if he had been using it to remove the traces of poison he would have filled the upper section as well. A small point perhaps but the witness could at least have been asked to confirm this. Also, according to Donellan, she was one of the servants working in the kitchen that he spoke to when he was looking for Samuel Frost to bring a ladder into the orchard, and if she had confirmed this it would have cast further doubt on Lady Boughton's testimony.

The Revd Newsam was the next witness, led through his evidence by Mr Digby, who concentrated on a single episode – the conversation with the prisoner on the Saturday prior to Theodosius's death. He had been away from home for the previous four months and Donellan told him that 'Sir Theodosius was in a very ill state of health, that he had never got rid of the disorder that he had brought with him from Eton, but rather in his opinion had been adding to it; that he had made such frequent use of mercury, inwardly and outwardly, that his blood was a mass of mercury and corruption; that he had a violent swelling in his groin, which they were endeavouring to bring to a head, but he was so obstinate that he would not live well enough to do it; that they were fearful it would return into his blood, for at this time it was at a crisis; that he had frequent swellings in his throat, and his breath was so offensive they could hardly sit at table with him; that his intellects at intervals were so much affected that nobody knew what it was to live with him.'

This catalogue of afflictions prompted Mr Newsam to respond sadly that if that was the case he did not think 'his life was worth two years' purchase', to which

Donellan replied, 'Not one.' However, he had not at that stage seen Theodosius since his return, and when he did so he was agreeably surprised. The young man did not look so 'florid' as he had done but otherwise 'he looked like a man to all appearance in health.'

The cross-examination by Mr Green was even briefer, with no attempt to dispute his account even though Donellan claimed that Mr Newsam had already seen Theodosius and actually initiated the conversation, expressing his concern about the youth's condition. He also asserted that Mr Newsam had confirmed this shortly afterwards whilst speaking to a Mr Clay from Rugby but the Defence team apparently saw no advantage in questioning him on this, let alone calling Mr Clay to support their client's contention. In view of the evidence he had just given, Mr Newsam would no doubt have disputed this, but Donellan had also stated that a short time later the Rector had actually confirmed his version.

Instead, Mr Green asked the Rector about a letter he had received from the accused on the morning of the exhumation. At Donellan's request, this had been put into the court but Counsel did not ask for it to be produced or even for its contents to be revealed, leaving the jury mystified as to why it had ever been raised.

In fact, Donellan had written the letter because he had heard that Mr Newsam, who had been as keen as anyone else in the neighbourhood to have the body opened, had invited Lord Denbeigh 'to dine with him that day, in order that his Lordship might exert his influence on the occasion.' Accordingly, 'not thinking that Mr Newsam was his enemy', he wrote to him, 'desiring that he would attend the inquest, and prevail upon Lord Denbeigh to attend with him likewise, meaning nothing more thereby than a wish to have his character cleared up, not only to Mr Newsam, but more materially to Lord Denbeigh, whose representation of it to the world might have had weight, and might have alleviated Mr Donellan, under so cruel and unjust an accusation, more than anything else.'

Mr Newsam replied immediately, assuring Donellan of his friendship and promising that he would 'consider the contents of his letter and communicate the same to Lord Denbeigh.' It was this same noble lord, of course, who had engaged in that private conversation with Lady Boughton immediately before the resumption of the Inquest, so it would seem that Donellan's faith in him as a supportive voice was sadly misplaced.

William Kerr, the surgeon from Northampton under whose care Theodosius had been placed when he first returned from Eton, was the next to take the oath and he was unequivocal in his view of the young man's state of health at that time:

Q. Was the disorder for which you attended him at that time completely cured or not?

A. I really saw no disorder; there was upon the prepuce or glands, I do not recollect which, a small wart or excrescence, very immaterial indeed. It was so slight that I did not consider it a subject of medicine at all. I ordered some lotion to wash it with, and nothing else, and dissuaded him from the use of medicine.

Q. Was the state of his body such that you judged it necessary to give him a prescription to take medicines by?

A. I gave him a prescription for the lotion, but none for internal medicines.

Q. When he went from under your care you considered him as by no means disordered?

A. I considered him as having no venereal complaint.

Faced with this confident assertion, the Defence might have questioned the witness on his experience of the ailment, particularly his awareness of the fact that a sufferer could frequently enjoy quite lengthy periods of remission before it reasserted itself. As it was though, Mr Newnham had just one question:

Q. In common parlance is not lotion a medicine?

A. Certainly.

But this hardly took the Defence case any further forward.

The Crown now moved on to the medical evidence concerning the aftermath of Theodosius's death and although he had not performed the actual autopsy Dr Rattray was the first to be called. Another member of the Prosecution team, Mr Balguy, began by taking him through his visit to the Hall, along with Mr Wilmer, on the evening of September 4th. He told how they were met by the accused who, as he ushered them into the parlour, asked if they had heard from or seen Sir William Wheler. They replied that they had not and Donellan added, 'I rather expect Sir William will be here, or if he does not come I shall hear from him.'

This would seem to be a point in his favour, and Counsel moved on swiftly, asking about the letter from Sir William that they were shown. This had apparently arrived while they were waiting for the coffin to be unsoldered, for when they returned to the entrance hall they surprised Mr Powell in the act of reading it, even though it was clearly addressed to Donellan. This was in fact the expected response by Sir William to his being urged to be present at that time, in which he said that he 'conceived no person was proper to be there but the surgeon and physician sent for.'

Probing further, Balguy asked if they had been informed of any other correspondence from Sir William and his witness described how, after searching in his waistcoat pocket, Donellan produced just the cover of a second letter, addressed in the baronet's hand. He told them that this earlier missive was written in the same 'exceeding polite' terms but did not go into any details of its content – even though, of course, as the Prosecution would show later, this was the letter that broached the possibility that Theodosius had been poisoned.

Dr Rattray then described how he and his colleagues went upstairs to Theodosius's room. 'Mr Wilmer went in first I believe; he came out of the room testifying some surprise as I entered the door. I immediately entered and saw the body for the first time... I went into the room and looked at the body several times and came out to Mr Wilmer. He seemed to think it would answer no purpose to open the body at that time, and as we asked Mr Donellan for what purpose it was to be opened and he said it was for the satisfaction of the family, we thought it at so late a period, and it being only for that purpose that it was no use, therefore we waived it.'

This seems clear enough, but Counsel was determined that this telling point was not lost on the jury, especially as the missing letter, in which Sir William declared that the sole purpose of an autopsy was to be seen to be responding to the rumours of poison, was going to be produced later on in the proceedings:

Q. Had Captain Donellan said the opening it was for the satisfaction of the family?

A. Yes. He told Mr Wilmer so, and I think when I went up the same speech was repeated to me.

Q. Did he mention any other purpose for which the body was to be opened except the satisfaction of the family?

A. None to me that I recollect.

Q. Did he at any time intimate to you any suspicion of poison?

A. No. Nothing of the sort.

Q. In consequence of this you did not in fact open the body?

A. We did not open the body.

Moving on to September 9th, Dr Rattray told how he was summoned to Newbold churchyard. 'I received a message by some strange roundabout way, in consequence of which I went, but I don't know who sent it.' He then gave his impression of the 'material appearances' of the body prior to its opening, the overall distended condition, the swollen face, 'extremely black, with the lips swelled and retracted, and showing the gums.' The tongue protruded between blackened teeth, with the blackness diminishing as it reached the breast. The body was slightly mottled in places – one of the most commonly cited signs of cyanide poisoning – and there was 'another circumstance which for decency I have omitted, but if called upon I am ready to mention.'

This was presumably related to Theodosius's venereal complaint but as the Prosecution's case was that this was negligible, Mr Balguy brushed it aside as being 'not at all material.' He moved on instead to the autopsy itself and Rattray told how 'the bowels in the lower belly seemed to put on the appearance of inflammation.' Being a stickler for accuracy, he felt it necessary to define exactly what he meant by this. 'I choose to make use of the vulgar term appearance, in order to convey a general idea of the appearance things in that state generally put on.' The inflammation had also affected the orifices of the stomach, but the heart seemed to be 'in its natural state.' The lungs, however, were suffused with blood, as was the diaphragm, while the kidneys 'appeared black as tinder, and the liver much in the same state.'

Counsel was now approaching the crux of the matter. Having ascertained that the witness had heard the testimony of Mr Powell and Lady Boughton, 'independent of appearances, for I would have you forget them for the present instant, what was in your judgement the occasion of Sir Theodosius's death?'

'Independent of appearances of the body,' came the reply, 'I am of opinion that the draught, in consequence of the symptoms which succeeded the swallowing of it, as described by Lady Boughton, was poison, and the immediate cause of his death.'

The second phial that had been earlier examined by Mr Powell was then passed to the witness.

'Please to smell upon that bottle,' invited Counsel. 'What in your judgement is the noxious medicine in that bottle?'

'I know the liquid well. It is a distillation of laurel leaves, commonly called laurel water.'

After confirming that in his opinion the prescription drawn up by the apothecary was perfectly 'innocent and proper', he described the experiments that he, together with Mr Wilmer and Mr Snow, had conducted on the dog and two horses, stressing how the autopsies had revealed the same inflammation, especially in the lungs, that he had observed in Theodosius's body, 'very different I believe from the natural colour.'

Lady Boughton had compared the smell of the potion she administered to that of bitter almonds, and he agreed that the bottle produced in court had that self-same effect, adding helpfully, 'I have given the laurel water to many people to smell to, and they always described the smell to be something like bitter almonds.'

Bringing his questioning to what should have been an inescapable conclusion, Counsel asked, 'In your judgement is the quantity that one of these bottles contain of laurel water sufficient to take away life from any human creature?' Back came the required response: 'In my opinion it is.' But instead of leaving it at that, Balguy felt impelled to underline this one more time.

'I have now got your opinion upon the subject, independent of any appearances you observed upon the body of Sir Theodosius Boughton. Now are you from these appearances confirmed, or otherwise, in the opinion you have given?'

He should have noted the danger signals in Rattray's fastidious definition of 'appearance' for he was clearly not prepared to commit himself if there was the slightest room for doubt. The most he could offer was that he was confirmed in his opinion 'so far as upon the viewing a body so long after the death of the subject one can be allowed to form a judgement upon such appearances.'

This qualification gave Mr Newnham, rising to cross-examine, the perfect opening:

Q. If I do not misunderstand you, Doctor, the last account you gave in answer to the question, whether you are confirmed in this opinion by the appearances, you said yes, so far as you might be allowed to form an opinion viewing the body so long after the death of the subject?

A. Yes, so far as we may be allowed to form a judgement upon appearances so long after death.

Q. By putting it in that way, do you or do you not mean to say that all judgement upon such a subject, in such a case, is unfounded?

But Rattray was not prepared to go that far. 'I cannot say that, because from the analogy between the appearances in that body and those distinguishable in animals killed by the poison I have mentioned, I think them so much alike that I am rather confirmed in my opinion with respect to the operation of the draught.'

There was, though, one crucial difference. 'Those bodies,' enquired Newnham, 'were instantly opened?'

'Yes,' came the acknowledgement, 'so much so that there was the peristaltick motion of the bowels upon their being pricked.'

And, driving home his advantage, Counsel continued, 'This was upon the eleventh day after Sir Theodosius's death?' To which Rattray replied simply, 'Yes.'

Encouraged by this, Newnham turned next to the visit to Lawford Hall on September 4th. Having established that the corpse was giving off a 'violent stench', being in an advanced state of putrefaction, he asked why, at that time, the doctors were not prepared to open the body.

'I have just said,' Rattray responded, with some irritation, 'the body seemed to us to be in such a very disagreeable state that we did not like to enter into the investigation of it, not knowing that any particular purpose was to be answered by it, except the satisfaction of the family.'

Donellan's failure to mention the suspicions of poison was, of course, a major weakness of his defence, and Newnham tried to divert attention from it:

Q. At that time was not you and Mr Wilmer sent for for the purpose of opening the body?

A. Yes; it was so expressed in the note.

Q. Was not your reason at that time (whether you were erroneous in your judgement or not, is another thing) but was not your reason for declining opening the body that you conceived the opening it could answer no useful purpose?

A. At that time we were of that opinion.

Newnham then returned to the matter of Sir William Wheler being apprised of the outcome of their visit and managed to establish another point in his client's favour. Rattray admitted that although, as he and Wilmer were leaving the Hall, Donellan asked if they would be seeing the baronet, he did not actually do so until after he received a letter from the accused two days later 'desiring me or Mr Wilmer, or both of us, to go to Sir William Wheler and inform him of the circumstances that happened at Lawford Hall on the night of the 4th.'

Turning to the exhumation which, he reminded the court, took place eleven days after Theodosius's death, Newnham asked, 'Does not putrefaction increase very much in the space of five or six days in a hot summer?' 'Very much' was going a little too far for the doctor's precise mind, but he had to agree that 'it must certainly increase.'

'Was not the body,' pursued Counsel, 'in a very high state of putrefaction when you saw it?' But once again, this was overstating the case in Rattray's estimation:

'Upon the shroud being removed, the body appeared to me much fairer than I expected. I expected to have seen it in a very black putrefied state, but the external appearance was not quite so highly so as I expected.'

His next quibble came when Counsel suggested that in his signed account of the examination, given at the Inquest, the appearances of the various organs are 'particularly described.'

'They are not particularly described,' protested Rattray. 'There is something said about the stomach and bowels.'

If then, pursued Newnham blandly, his investigation was so limited, what was the point of his attending the autopsy? Stung by this, the witness responded, 'I did not know that it was necessary before a coroner's jury to enter into the particulars.' He went on ingenuously, 'I was quite a novice in the business.'

Deliberately, one feels, misunderstanding this, Counsel asked mischievously, 'Do you mean a novice in the mode of dissection?'

'No,' retorted Rattray. 'In the business before a coroner.'

Still pursuing the matter of the external appearance of the body, Newnham wondered whether the swelling of the features might not be a sign of putrefaction. Rattray's careful response, 'I really don't know that they are' provided the opportunity for another attempt to undermine his air of authority.

'I do not mean to give you any offence,' Counsel assured him in his smoothest manner, 'but I beg leave to ask whether you have been much used to anatomical dissection.'

'I have been,' replied the doctor stiffly, 'as far as persons not particularly intended for anatomical pursuits. I am not a professor of anatomy.'

But this did not satisfy Counsel, and his enquiry, 'Did you ever attend the dissection of a human body that was poisoned, or suspected to have been poisoned?' elicited the single word response, 'Never.'

Turning to the appearance of the abdomen, Newnham again seemed to be setting out to rile the witness. 'Not being an anatomical man,' he confessed, straight-faced, 'it has slipped my memory. Will you please to repeat it?'

When Rattray reiterated the signs of inflammation in the stomach and bowels, Counsel suggested that it too might be the result of putrefaction but this was firmly rejected. Newnham did though extract the admission that because the stench was so offensive the bowels were not examined in detail and this allowed him to ask, 'Are not the bowels the seat of poison?' Having obtained agreement on this, he continued, 'Then why did not you examine into the contents of the bowels?' and to this all that the witness could say was, 'I did not think it in the power of anyone to examine into the contents of the bowels, their contents being so strong and disagreeable.'

Rattray's initial conclusion, based on the symptoms described by Lady Boughton, had been that Theodosius had died from arsenical poisoning, but he now believed that he was mistaken. Newnham seized on this admission: if he was wrong at first, why might he not be wrong now? And beyond repeating his conviction that this time his analysis was correct, the doctor had no answer to this.

Immediately after the autopsy, Donellan had told Catherine Amos that he believed that Theodosius's death was caused by a broken blood vessel, and Newnham raised this as a possibility, referring the witness back to his description of the unusual amount of blood on both sides of the lungs. With Rattray conceding that the rupture of a blood vessel could occasion death, he raised the possibility of the convulsions that both Lady Boughton and Catherine Amos had described being so extreme because a blood vessel had been fractured, but the witness would not go that far, declaring firmly, 'It is a case I am not supposing probable.' If not probable, asked Counsel, is it at least possible? 'Everything,' came the unanswerable response, 'is possible under God.'

With the death of Theodosius's father in his mind, Newnham took the convulsions a stage further. Were they not, he suggested, a symptom of either apoplexy or an epileptic fit? But once again, Rattray would not concede this, declaring that in his opinion they were entirely the result of the draught that Lady Boughton had administered.

In an attempt to regain the initiative, Newnham returned to Rattray's original diagnosis, asking why he had first suspected arsenic. But this merely gave the doctor the chance to come across as a reliable witness, doing his best to give a balanced view of the affair, with his frank admission that, 'Every man is mistaken now and then in his opinion, and that was my case. I am not ashamed to own a mistake.'

Moving on to the experiments carried out with Wilmer and Snow, Counsel attempted to undermine the findings, arguing that there would be crucial differences between the effects of poison on animals and human beings. But Rattray disagreed strongly and Newnham was forced to conclude his cross-examination by returning yet again to what he hoped was the much stronger point of the doctor's mistaken attribution of the cause of death to arsenic.

However, labouring it in this way merely suggested that the Defence was clutching at straws, and with the briefest of re-examinations Mr Balguy came back to an area where the accused was on much shakier ground. Referring to the abandoned examination on September 4th, he asked, 'If at that time Captain

Donellan had insinuated to you any suspicion of poison, would you or not have taken the shroud from the body?'

And, given the chance to leave the witness stand on a much stronger note, the doctor replied stoutly, 'I verily believe, had I known the tendency of the enquiry I should have sat there for a month rather than have left the body unopened.'

Rather than allowing this to be the last word though, Newnham rose again to put just one more question: would the witness confirm that when the body was opened its external appearance made no contribution to the assessment of the cause of death? Doctor Rattray readily agreed but even so it could be said that in reality, despite all Defence Counsel's best efforts to destabilise this key witness, the Crown had had the last word.

Chapter Twelve

MR BRADFORD Wilmer was the next witness to be sworn but as his evidence covered much the same ground as his colleague's both the Prosecution and Defence dealt with him much more briefly. Mr Wheeler, given the chance to make up for his inept performance earlier, began with the visit to Lawford Hall on September 4th, and his witness confirmed that 'the body was so extremely putrid that I declared my opinion to Dr Rattray that the proposed enquiry could give no sort of information.' Even so, if he had been aware of any thought of poison he would have gone ahead with the autopsy.

He also confirmed Rattray's account of the experiments on the greyhound and the mare and agreed with his colleague that the effect of laurel water on the human body would be fatal. Shown the phial that had already been produced, he declared, 'I imagine one bottle of that size full of laurel water would be sufficient to kill in half an hour's time any man in this court.'

Cross-examined by Mr Green he said that when the autopsy was finally performed there were about two pints of blood in the stomach region and he conceded that such a loss of blood could cause convulsions. Asked whether Donellan had, on either the 4th or 9th of September, shown any reluctance to have the body opened, he replied, 'Not the least in the world… I believe it was at his own request that a man was sent for to unsolder the coffin.'

He also acknowledged hearing the accused ask Dr Rattray if he would be seeing Sir William Wheler and thought that his colleague had said that he would visit him the next day and 'give him an account of the business.'

Once again, the Crown took immediate steps to undermine any favourable impression made by the Defence, and Mr Wheeler rose to ask just a single but crucial supplementary question: based on the appearance of the body and the testimony of other witnesses, to what did he attribute the victim's death? Back came the unequivocal response: 'After having heard Lady Boughton's evidence, and therefore being acquainted with the symptoms which preceded the death of Sir Theodosius Boughton, I am clearly of opinion that his death was occasioned by a poisonous draught administered to him by Lady Boughton on the morning of his death.'

Next to take the stand were two more medical witnesses: Dr Ashe, physician, from Birmingham and Dr Parsons, Professor of Anatomy at the University of Oxford. Neither could speak from personal experience of the present case but both were acknowledged experts in their fields. They agreed with the previous witnesses that from the symptoms immediately prior to Theodosius's death, he had been poisoned. Dr Parsons was questioned in some detail about the possibility of the convulsions being brought on by either epilepsy or apoplexy but he firmly rejected both.

'Then your judgement is,' asked Mr Howarth, 'that the fatal effects were produced by the medicine thus taken?'

'I think there can be no doubt of that,' the Professor replied, 'as they commenced almost as soon as he swallowed the draught; and a mixture such as he is supposed to have taken is known to have the power of producing them.'

The Defence though was still clinging to the alternative possibilities and Mr Newnham enquired if he had never known, 'instances of persons being taken suddenly when engaged in pleasure or business or at dinner and dying convulsed epileptic or apoplectic?'

Professor Parsons admitted that he had, 'but those who die suddenly of apoplexy are generally persons of a full habit, and who are neither so thin nor so young as Sir Theodosius Boughton.'

Had he never though, pursued Counsel, 'heard of a person having the appearance of perfect health being seized with an epilepsy without any primary cause giving any warning? Have you never heard of people in perfect health being felled with an epilepsy or apoplexy?'

Dr Parsons acknowledged that he had, and that the latter could arise from 'the sudden bursting of a blood vessel.' But, he added firmly, although this was possible, 'I think there is no reason to go so far for a cause as to *possibility*, when this medicine as all the world knows will effect it.' This though, continued Mr Newnham, was assuming that the baronet had in fact swallowed two ounces of laurel water. Far less, came the riposte, would be 'sufficient for the purpose.' But he had to admit that his identification of laurel water was based solely on the smell of bitter almonds that had been reported.

'Will not black cherry water have that smell?' asked Counsel.

It does, agreed the Professor, but, he went on, 'it is now out of use. I do not suppose there is an apothecary in the land who has it, and therefore it could not be substituted by accident for the other vehicle.' Even so, the Defence had made some significant inroads into his evidence, but once more Mr Newnham went one question too far, asking, 'Will not bitter almonds have that smell?'

If he had done his homework more thoroughly he could have anticipated the inevitable response: 'Yes. And spirits flavoured with them are said to be poisonous to the human species.'

As at the Inquest, Samuel Bucknill was the last medical witness to be called by the Crown, an indication perhaps that his manner would not go down well with the jury. Certainly, he betrayed his pomposity with the very first exchange with Mr Balguy:

Q. I believe you are a surgeon?

A. I profess surgery.

Asked about his two visits to Lawford Hall, the first being on the day after that of the two Coventry physicians, he recalled the prisoner's response to his offer to carry out the autopsy, or at the very least remove the dead man's stomach. Donellan rejected this, saying that as Dr Rattray and Mr Wilmer had decided against opening the body, it would not be right 'to do anything after men so eminent in their profession' ('as he expressed himself,' inserted Bucknill gratuitously) 'had declined it.'

However, instructed by Sir William Wheler, he returned to the Hall the next day, where he was to meet with Mr Snow, Sir William's personal physician. Bucknill arrived first and there then followed the chapter of missed opportunities when, with Snow not yet arrived, he was called away to attend a sick patient.

'I had not rode above a mile from Lawford Hall,' he declared, 'when I heard a person calling after me who was on a full gallop. He told me Mr Snow was come. I dare say I could not have gone three minutes before Mr Snow came. I told the person I would be back in an hour but could not return back then as I had received a message from a patient who in all probability was dying.'

He did return within the hour, only to find that Snow had gone, leaving instructions that the burial should proceed without further delay. Donellan apologised for his having been put to 'all this unnecessary trouble' and, Bucknill concluded, 'I took my horse and rode away as fast as I could.' Both sets of lawyers seem to have been conscious of time passing, for although he had been the one to

finally perform the autopsy his testimony ended at this point and the Defence chose
not to cross-examine him.

Instead, the Crown moved on to the remaining Hall servants, starting with the
coachman, William Frost. He gave a vivid account of the events on the morning of
Theodosius's death, describing it, as he assured the court, 'as near as I possibly
can.' The Captain and my Lady, he said, 'were to go to the Wells to drink the
water. They ordered me to get the horses ready; I got them ready near about seven
in the morning; I took them to the gate. Captain Donellan came out to the gate and
felt the horse girths. He said, "Are they fast, William?" I said, "They are." He said,
"I will go and see if my Lady is ready." He came back and said, "My Lady is not
ready yet. I will take my mare and go to the Wells." I took the horses in. When I
had been in the stable a considerable time, Lady Boughton came and called,
"William!" I said, "My Lady." She said, "You must go to Mr Powell and fetch him
as fast as possible. My son is dangerously ill." I said there was none but her horse
in the stable. She said that would not go fast enough. I must get the mare. I told
her Captain Donellan had the mare. She bid me go and meet him and take the
mare. I shut the door and went towards the gate; the Captain came inside the gate;
I told him I was to go to Mr Powell. Captain Donellan made some answer but
what it was I did not take particular notice. I took the mare and went.'

Mr Digby, for the Crown, then asked if, on his return, he had been called into
the parlour by the accused. The intention, of course, was to confirm Lady
Boughton's story of Donellan's immediate anxiety to establish an alibi, but his
witness, stickler for accuracy that he was, was not so sure. 'I was called into the
parlour by Captain Donellan, but whether it was the same morning, or a morning
or two after, I cannot recollect.' In other words, the incident could have occurred
later than Lady Boughton claimed, by which time rumours of foul play were
already beginning to swirl round Donellan. The coachman went on to quote the
accused as saying, 'William, which gate did I come out at that morning?' *That*,
rather than *this*, implies a later date, as does his conclusion that '*afterwards*, he said
I should be a clear evidence for him about his coming out at that gate.'

The Defence could have picked this up as further evidence of the fallibility of
Lady Boughton's testimony but opted not to cross-examine. In any case, Donellan's
apparent desire to distance himself from the giving of the fatal potion was
misplaced for, as Mr Justice Buller had pointed out in his initial Charge, if it could
be proved that the accused was responsible for the presence of the poison, his not
actually administering it was irrelevant.

The next witness, young Samuel Frost, had collected the final concoction from Mr Powell and delivered it directly to Sir Theodosius, who immediately took it upstairs. He was fishing with his master from seven o'clock in the evening until his return to the Hall at dusk and in all that time did not see the accused. The jury did not need reminding that Lady Boughton had said that Donellan told her, when he joined her in the garden, that he had been to the river to try and persuade her son to come back to the Hall. Sir Theodosius, the witness continued, had remained on horseback the whole time and because he was wearing boots could not have wet his feet – whatever, was the clear implication, Donellan might have said to the contrary.

Next morning, he woke his master at six in order to get the straps he needed to repair the fishing nets, and at this time 'he appeared in a very good state of health.' In his few minutes on the witness stand, Samuel had strengthened the Crown's case considerably and accordingly the Defence opted to cross-examine.

Donellan had of course provided them with a totally different account of his movements on the evening prior to Theodosius's death and, as he had pointed out to them, he would never have claimed to have been to the river when such an assertion could be so easily disproved. But as he had no chance to challenge Lady Boughton's version in person, the best that Defence Counsel Dayrell could achieve was to establish that Theodosius was already fishing when Samuel joined him, some two hours after delivering the medicine. In other words, it must have been later than seven o'clock, thus leaving open the possibility that Donellan could have been to the river and left again before the servant arrived.

Mr Dayrell turned to the potions that Samuel had delivered:

Q. Did your master complain that the physic Mr Powell had sent him before made him sick?

A. I never heard him make any complaint of it.

Q. Did not you tell Mr Powell so?

A. Not that physic. He never said anything to me about it.

Q. Did he about any physic?

A. No, not to me.

Mr Dayrell though had not missed the qualification. 'What did you mean,' he asked, 'by saying not *that* physic?'

'He took one dose of physic,' Samuel admitted, 'which made him very ill, and he brought it up again.' And as with the older Frost, he showed his anxiety to stick to the literal truth, adding, 'But he did not mention anything to me about it.'

Mary Lynes, former maid to Theodosia, came next and from the outset Mr Wheeler found her heavy going. She had, she said, already left the Hall by the time of Theodosius's death:

Q. When did you leave it?

A. I cannot tell justly when I did leave it.

Q. Was it a month or six weeks before Sir Theodosius's death?

A. About a month before, I believe.

Q. How long had you lived there before you left that place?

A. I cannot justly tell.

Q. Did you live there a twelvemonth or half a year?

A. No.

Q. Might you have been there three or four months?

A. I might.

Abandoning this unproductive line, Counsel moved on to the crux of her evidence. Did she, he asked, know anything about a still? Yes, she did. 'Mention what you know about it,' invited Mr Wheeler.

'I will tell the truth and nothing else,' his witness replied virtuously. 'Mr Donellan distilled roses. I do not know that he distilled anything else.'

This was not exactly helpful to the Prosecution's case, but Counsel pressed on:

Q. Where was the still kept?

A. In what he called his own room.

Q. Was that the room he slept in?

A. No, he did not sleep there.

Q. Was the door of that room locked?

A. He slept there when Madam Donellan was brought to bed, but at no time else while I was there.

Q. Was that room locked in which the still was?

A. It was kept locked before Mrs Donellan was brought to bed, but when she was brought to bed it was open.

Q. Do you know anything of his using this still frequently?

A. Yes, distilling roses. I do not know that he distilled anything else.

Having seen the tangle Mr Wheeler had got himself into, the Defence chose to let her evidence stand, so the Crown called the last of the Hall servants, the gardener, Francis Amos. But he too was to prove less than satisfactory for their cause.

He had also, he said, been 'a fishing' with his master the night before he died.

'Was Mr Donellan fishing with him?' asked Mr Howarth – a carefully phrased question in view of the servants' clear determination to adhere to their oaths to tell 'nothing but the truth', without elaboration. This way, there was no risk of the witness saying that the accused had merely come to the river to speak to Theodosius, as he claimed.

Whether Amos was in fact so addicted to the truth though is open to doubt for he then recounted the story of Donellan's jovial words on the very day of Theodosius's death: 'Now, gardener, you shall live at your ease and work at your ease; it shall not be as it was in Sir Theodosius's days. I wanted before to be master but I have got master now, and shall be master.'

Amos too had something to say about the still. The accused brought it to him two or three days after Theodosius's death to be cleaned as it was full of wet lime, which Donellan said he had used to kill fleas. Hoping for a more positive answer than the previous witness had given, Counsel asked, 'You, as gardener, I suppose, know whether he used to gather things in the garden for the purpose of distilling?'

But this just elicited the grudging response, 'He might, for what I know.'

Undeterred, Mr Howarth ploughed on. 'Have you ever got anything?'

'I have got lavender for him to distil and have taken it into the house.'

Still, then, no confirmation of Donellan's use of laurel leaves, so Counsel tried again. 'Have you,' he enquired hopefully, 'in your garden any laurel trees?'

'Yes. And bays too – and laureltinus,' Amos added helpfully – or very possibly unhelpfully, for he must have known that the latter is a member of the vibernum family and, despite the similarity of name, has no affinity with laurel.

'And celery?' interposed Mr Newnham, tongue perhaps in cheek.

'Yes,' came the reply, but quite how this was of benefit to the Defence is not clear. It is true that celery was the source of a diuretic used in the treatment of gout, from which Donellan suffered, but without elucidation this would have been lost on the jury.

Amos concluded his evidence by recounting another conversation with the prisoner that took place on the morning that Theodosius died. 'He said, "Gardener, you must go and take a couple of pigeons directly." I said there were none fit to eat. He said, "It will make no odds if they are not, for they are for Sir Theodosius. We must have them ready against the doctor comes. Poor fellow!" says he. "He lies in a sad agony now with this damned nasty distemper, the pox. It will be the death of him.".' (The use of pigeons in this way was a long-held remedy, referred to by the seventeenth century playwright John Webster in *The Duchess of Malfi*: 'I would sooner eat a dead pigeon taken from the soles of the feet of one sick of the plague than kiss one of you fasting.') However, continued Amos, on entering the house with the pigeons, 'I met my Lady and Madam Donellan at the door; they were wringing their hands. They said, "It is too late now. He is dead." They sent me for two women to lay him out.'

Despite the near incredibility of Amos's story of his other conversation with Donellan, the Defence chose not to cross-examine and the next witness, William Crofts was called. He had been a member of the Inquest jury and he told how, during Lady Boughton's evidence concerning the rinsing of the bottles, he saw 'Captain Donellan catch her by the gown and give her a twitch.' According to Donellan this incident occurred, not at that precise moment, but earlier, when he misheard her and thought she had confused her daughter with her daughter's maid, but the Defence, with their lack of trust in their client's word, saw no point in putting forward this alternative version and did not cross-examine.

They did though make some attempt to undermine the credibility of the next witness, John Darbyshire. He, it will be recalled, had shared a cell with the accused and had been told by Sukey Sparrow that she believed he was innocent. But, having interviewed him, the Defence solicitors had advised against calling him for they had found him a shifty character who would not stand up well to cross-examination.

However, questioned by Mr Digby for the Crown, he recounted a conversation he claimed to have had with the prisoner:

'We were both in one room together; he had a bed in the same room I had for a month or five weeks, I believe. In our conversation in the prison I used to tell Captain Donellan what I had heard. I remember one time we had a conversation about Sir Theodosius Boughton's being poisoned. I asked Captain Donellan whether the body was poisoned or not. He said there was no doubt of it. I said, "For God's sake, Captain, who could do it?" He said it was done amongst themselves; he had no hand in it; he had nothing to do with it. I asked him who he meant by themselves. He said himself, Lady Boughton, the footman and the apothecary.'

'Who did he mean,' asked Counsel, 'by himself?'

'Sir Theodosius Boughton. I said, "Sure he could not do it himself." He said no, he did not think he did; he could not believe he would. I told him I thought the apothecary could hardly do it for he had no interest in it, he would lose a good patient. That his footman could have no interest in it, and it was very unnatural to suppose that Lady Boughton would do it.'

Unprompted, Darbyshire then had a strange tale to tell: 'He then spoke of Lady Boughton, how covetous she was. He said she had received an anonymous letter the day after Sir Theodosius's death, charging her plump with poisoning Sir Theodosius; that she had called him and read it to him and she trembled, he said. She desired he would not let his wife know of that letter, and asked him if he would give up his right to the personal estate, and some estates of about two hundred pounds a year belonging to the family. I think that was the substance of that conversation.'

Nothing more was said about this mysterious letter, and as Donellan had previously renounced any rights to his wife's possessions, the latter point was of very doubtful value. Mr Newnham, leading for the Defence, questioned him at some length. According to his client, the two had fallen out when he, Donellan, refused to lend him money, and it was immediately after this that Darbyshire had contacted Mr Caldecott to offer his services to the Prosecution. It would not be the first – or last – time that a prisoner has given evidence against a cell-mate, either in revenge for some slight or in the hope of favourable treatment, and Counsel set out to make clear to the court the witness's unreliability:

Q. What way of life was you in before you came to this gaol?

A. A tradesman, and a very reputable one.

Q. Not a successful tradesman?

A. I have failed.

Q. How often?

A. Twice, the more is my misfortune.

Q. Do you mean twice a bankrupt?

A. Yes, but I fell fairly.

Mr Newnham then introduced the names of two other individuals:

Q. You know Mr Pope very well?

A. Yes.

Q. And Sir Alexander Leith too?

A. I did not know him.

Q. But you did know Mr Pope?

A. Yes, I did. But not Sir Alexander Leith. I never spoke to Sir Alexander in my life.

This was a reference to a scandal originating in Darbyshire's home town of Birmingham, and one that would almost certainly have been familiar to the jury.

Mr Pope had launched a private prosecution against Sir Alexander Leith, which he not only lost but found himself countersued for libel and ordered to pay damages of ten thousand pounds. Pope had in consequence absconded, leaving the money unpaid. Darbyshire had been his principal adviser in the original case, which had been heard before none other than Mr Justice Buller.

Aware of the effect of all this on the jury, Mr Howarth once again contrived to have the last word, returning to Donellan's insistence that Theodosius had been poisoned. He had, apparently, held this view since at least Christmas, in other words several months into his confinement and an indication that by then he had had to accept this and abandon his earlier efforts to suggest alternative causes for the victim's death.

The final witness for the Crown was Sir William Wheler, and his principal function was to identify the correspondence that passed between himself and Donellan after the death of his ward. The letters were shown to him before being read aloud and he confirmed that the ones he had received were in Donellan's hand. The crucial letter that he had written on September 4th, after first hearing the rumours of poison and which Donellan had failed to show Rattray and Wilmer, was still missing but Sir William had recreated it from memory, including the vital words, 'I assure you that it is reported, all over the country, that he was killed either by medicine or by poison. The country will never be convinced to the contrary unless the body is opened, and we shall be very much blamed.'

As regards Donellan's letter of September 5th in which, reporting on the first visit of the physicians, he wrote, 'I am happy to inform you that they fully satisfied us,' Sir William declared that he did not 'entertain any idea but that the body had been opened.'

There was very little the Defence could do about this, but Mr Newnham did question him about the death of Theodosius's father. Asked if he recollected what he died of, Sir William replied, 'He died suddenly, but I don't know what of.'

'I believe,' continued Counsel, 'he died as he was walking home,' and the witness agreed that this was so.

The clear implication was that father and son had died of similar causes, and Mr Howarth rose, determined to quash that particular line:

Q. What sort of person was the late Sir Edward Boughton?

A. A short, thick-set, fat man.

Q. What sort of person was the late Sir Theodosius?

A. He was very thin, and was taller than his father.

To conclude the Crown's case, one further letter was entered into the court and read aloud – the one that Donellan had written to the Coroner and jury at the Inquest, and which Mr Howarth had already read in full during his opening address. The Crown also tried to introduce the letter sent by Donellan to Theodosia from prison but after a tussle between the opposing lawyers the judge ruled that this was inadmissible – although, of course, despite Mr Newnham's earlier objection, it had already been read out and made much of in Howarth's preamble.

Chapter Thirteen

IT WAS late afternoon by now, the court had been sitting with barely a break for upwards of eight hours and the Defence had not yet opened its case. The Prosecution had called nearly all of the witnesses who had given evidence at the Inquest, the exceptions being Sarah Blundell, who was of course dead, Mr Snow, who had played the least significant role of all the local medical men, Sarah Steane, who had laid out the body, and Thomas Hewitt, the miller from Rugby who had delivered Mr Bucknill's concoction to Theodosius two months before his death.

None of these would have added anything of note to the Crown's case, but all three could have made points in favour of the accused. Bernard Snow could have confirmed the putrid state of the body and, more importantly, that he, on his own initiative, had recommended to Donellan that the burial should take place without further delay. Sarah Steane could have stated that the corpse was in no worse a state than any of the others she had dealt with, and Hewitt's evidence would have reinforced the impression that Theodosius's health was causing concern before Powell was called in – and of course Bucknill had not been questioned about his potion, or anything else about his involvement with the baronet prior to his death. But, having rejected nearly all of Donellan's suggestions, the Defence was calling just three witnesses, only one of whom was of any real consequence.

They began though in traditional fashion with the 'Prisoner's Defence'. At that time, the Defence was denied the luxury of a direct address to the court by Counsel, and it was the end of the next century before the accused himself would be allowed to take the stand. All that Donellan was permitted was the presentation of a written defence to be read aloud, but this suffered two major disadvantages. It had been prepared in advance so he was unable to counter any of the assertions made during the actual trial and it was read on his behalf by the Clerk of the Arraigns, in no doubt a rapid monotone.

Donellan began by declaring that his marriage to Theodosia 'was with the entire approbation of her friends and guardians.' As with so many of his assertions whenever he found himself in trouble, this was to say the least 'economical with the *actualité*', as was his claim that 'ever since my marriage, the deceased and myself lived in perfect friendship and cordiality'. He was on firmer ground though with his statement that on several occasions he had rescued his brother-in-law from life-threatening situations.

The rest of his 'Defence' was devoted to the events between Theodosius's death and his burial, putting as positive a gloss as he could on his letters to Sir William and the thwarted attempts to open the body. His plea is a curiously truncated affair, with whole swathes of the Crown's case, especially his possession of a still and supposed behaviour on the fatal morning, ignored. He did in fact have arguments to make in his favour – whether convincing or not – on both these points, and the suspicion arises that his lawyers cut short his address in order not to delay the court's proceedings any longer than was strictly necessary.

Instead, the 'Defence' moved swiftly to its conclusion, averring that: 'the most trifling actions and expressions have been handled to my prejudice; my private letters have been broke open, and many other unjustifiable steps have been taken to prejudice the world and embitter my defence. However, depending on the conscience of my judge and the unprejudiced impartiality of my jury, I trust my honour will be protected by their verdict.'

Two witnesses were then called to give their brief accounts of Donellan's apparent concern for Theodosius's welfare. Andrew Miller, the Rugby post-master and former proprietor of the Bear Inn, with its Assembly Room, told how the accused, having been sent for by Theodosius, intervened between him and Mr Wildgoose, acting 'in such a manner as to prevent their fighting.'

Another Rugby resident, George Loggie, testified that he was present when the young baronet picked a quarrel with the previous witness. When a clergyman, the Revd Chartres, came between them, 'Mr Miller asked pardon and Sir Theodosius forgave Mr Miller; then Sir Theodosius insisted upon fighting Mr Chartres. In consequence of that, Sir Theodosius sent for Captain Donellan; the Captain came over the next morning in consequence of the letter and interfered as a mediator.' Neither witness was cross-examined but in any case both incidents had occurred at least a year before Theodosius's death, by which time Donellan's attitude could have changed drastically.

The Defence then unveiled their one and only big gun – Mr John Hunter, surgeon by appointment to King George III and the most eminent anatomist of the time. He is considered today to be 'the father of modern surgery', and was the very man at whose feet Samuel Bucknill claimed to have sat.

However distinguished he might have been though, in the present situation he suffered from three major disadvantages. He had never previously been called to testify in a murder trial where poison was the alleged instrument; he had not been present at the exhumation and autopsy carried out on the victim; and finally, although the two expert witnesses called by the Crown had also been required to express an opinion at second-hand, they had supported the local men.

A Warwickshire jury, imbued no doubt with the very English trait of suspicion of so-called experts, would be far less receptive of the views of this outsider, with his outlandish Glaswegian accent, brought up from London to challenge the opinions of their own home-grown physicians.

Nevertheless, Mr Newnham sought to impress on them the fact that the individual whose views they were about to hear was no mere 'country practitioner'.

'You have been long in the habit of dissecting human subjects?' he enquired. 'I presume you have dissected more than any man in Europe?'

'I have dissected some thousands,' responded the witness grandly, 'during these thirty-three years.'

Drawing on this experience, he had no hesitation in declaring that the symptoms evident from the autopsy were 'entirely' due to putrefaction. Referring to the evidence of Lady Boughton on her son's reaction to the potion she gave him, Newnham asked if this was necessarily the result of poison, and back came the emphatic response, 'Certainly not.'

'If an apoplexy had come on,' continued Counsel, moving on to the Defence's alternative explanation for the tragedy, 'would not the symptoms have been nearly or somewhat similar?'

'Very much the same,' agreed Hunter.

The Crown had argued that Theodosius's youth undermined this theory, so Newnham tackled this head-on: 'Have you ever known or heard of a young subject dying of an apoplectic or epileptic fit?'

'Certainly.' This time though the witness felt constrained to modify this a little. 'But with regard to the apoplexy not so frequent. Young subjects will perhaps die more frequently of epilepsies than old ones; children are dying every day from teething, which is a species of epilepsy arising from an irritation.'

No, he replied to the next question, in all his years of practice he had never come across an instance of laurel water being given to a human being. His elaboration on this, however, was not so helpful. Speaking from his own experience, 'which is not a very confined one, because I have poisoned some thousands of animals', he declared that the results of poison on 'an animal of the brute creation' would be similar to the effects on a man.

Rather than labour this point, Counsel moved on to the dissection in question – carried out, although Hunter was presumably unaware of this, by one of his own disciples. He had two major criticisms: if poison was suspected, the 'guts' should have been examined and, because apoplexy was the far more likely cause of death, 'I wish in this case the head had been opened to remove all doubts.'

Summing up, Newnham returned to the key point: 'Then in your judgement upon the appearances the gentlemen have described, no inference can be drawn from thence that Sir Theodosius Boughton died of poison?'

And the response seemed to leave no room for doubt: 'Certainly not. It does not give the least suspicion.'

Nevertheless, Mr Howarth, rising to cross-examine, decided to probe a little further:

> 'Having heard, before today, that a person, apparently in health had swallowed a draught which had produced the symptoms described, I ask you whether any reasonable man can entertain a doubt that that draught, whatever it was, produced those appearances?'
>
> Although this was an apparently straightforward question, Mr Hunter could only reply, 'I don't know well what answer to make to that question.'
>
> Pouncing on this indecision, Counsel repeated it, this time making the link with Theodosius inescapable:

'I will therefore ask your opinion: having heard the account given of the health of this young gentleman on that morning, previous to taking the draught, and the symptoms that were produced immediately upon taking that draught, I ask your opinion, as a man of judgement, whether you do not think that draught was the occasion of his death?'

The witness could cope well enough with the first part of the question. 'With regard to his being in health, that explains nothing,' he declared firmly. 'I frequently, and indeed generally, see the healthiest people die suddenly.' But, he admitted, 'as to the circumstances of the draught, I own there are suspicions. Every man is just as good a judge as I am.'

However, this sudden onset of modesty does not seem to have impressed the judge, who broke in with the admonishment, 'You are to give your opinion upon the simple evidence, not taking in all the other evidence. Only speak upon the symptoms'

Unaccustomed to such a public reprimand, the learned doctor gave, as Blanchard noted in his shorthand record, 'no immediate answer.' The intervention certainly seems to have unsettled him still further especially when, breaking into the silence, Mr Howarth attempted for a third time to elicit a response: 'Upon the symptoms immediately produced upon the swallowing of that draught, I ask your judgement and opinion whether that draught did not occasion his death?'

With the brief initiative he had established draining away before his eyes, Mr Newnham intervened. 'I beg to object to that question, if it is put in that form. If it is put after the swallowing it, I have no objection.'

Quite what this quibble would achieve is not clear, and Mr Howarth happily complied: 'Then, *after* swallowing it, what is your opinion, allowing he had swallowed it?'

And the witness had finally to acknowledge that, 'I can only say that it is a circumstance in favour of such an opinion.'

This, at last, seems clear enough, but Mr Justice Buller intervened again, just to be absolutely sure: 'The symptoms as appeared afterwards are a circumstance in favour of an opinion the draught occasioned his death?'

But Hunter, remembering perhaps that he had been called to support the Defence, gave the bewildering reply, 'No, my Lord, because the symptoms afterwards are those of a man dying who was before in perfect health. A man dying of an epilepsy or apoplexy, or a thousand other sorts of disorders, the symptoms will give one those general ideas.'

Doing his best, one assumes, to keep the exasperation out of his voice, the judge tried again: 'It is the general idea you are asked about now, from the symptoms which appeared upon Sir Theodosius Boughton immediately after he took the draught, followed by his death so very soon after, whether, upon that part of the case, you are of opinion that the draught was the occasion of his death?'

Hunter, trying desperately to clamber out of the hole he had dug himself into, replied, 'If I was clear the draught was poison, or something obnoxious, I should say, most probably, that the symptoms arose from that. But when I first of all don't know that the draught was noxious, and I can conceive a number of other circumstances can kill, or produce the same effect, I cannot speak positively to it.'

Despite the transparent frankness of this response, it gave Mr Howarth the chance to put the most negative gloss on it: 'Then you decline giving any opinion upon the subject?'

'I cannot form an opinion upon the subject.'

'You refuse giving an opinion upon the subject, whether the death of Sir Theodosius Boughton was occasioned by the draught or not?'

Defence Counsel raising no objection to such emotive language, his star witness was left to give the honest but, to the jury, no doubt wholly inadequate reply, 'I cannot. I can conceive, if he had the draught of poison, the effects might arise from it; and I can conceive it might arise from other causes.'

Mr Howarth turned next to the effects of distilled laurel water, and the surgeon stated that as far as this was concerned in all of the experiments he had conducted on animals the fatal effects had not been nearly so instantaneous as had occurred with Sir Theodosius. In some instances, in fact, the creatures had survived.

'But you admit,' pressed Counsel, 'that laurel water would have produced symptoms such as have been described?' And Hunter had to agree that, 'I can conceive it might.'

Mr Newnham, with the whole of the Defence case in tatters, intervened once more, in a last-ditch effort to retrieve his witness's earlier self-assurance: 'Would not an apoplexy or an epilepsy, if it had seized Sir Theodosius Boughton at this time, though he had taken no physic at all, have produced similar symptoms too?' To which the doctor gratefully responded, 'Certainly.'

But then, having reminded the court that Sir Theodosius's father had died of an apoplexy, and having followed this with the simple question, 'Is not that a disease sometimes apt to run in the family?' Defence Counsel unleashed a mini-dissertation that would surely have left the jury totally confused: 'Where a father has died of an apoplexy,' he asked, 'is not that understood, in some measure, to be constitutional?'

'There is no disease whatever, that becomes constitutional, but what can be given to a child,' Mr Hunter declared. 'There is no disease which is acquired that can be given to a child, but whatever is constitutional in the father, the father has a power of giving that to the children. By which means it becomes what is called hereditary. There is no such thing as hereditary disease, but there is an hereditary disposition for a disease.'

In the baffled silence that followed, Mr Howarth took over once more, with another seemingly straightforward question: 'Do you call apoplexy constitutional?'

'I can easily conceive there are no diseases hereditary but what are constitutional. The small-pox is constitutional, though it require an immediate cause to produce the effect. The venereal disease is hereditary for that reason. I can easily conceive some constitutions are more disposed to an apoplexy than others.'

Once again, the Defence failed to follow up the reference to the hereditary nature of venereal disease, either in deference to Lady Boughton or perhaps because Hunter seemed to contradict the assertion in his previous reply that there is no such thing as a hereditary disease, but in any case the judge brought the questioning to an end with one final attempt to get a straight answer to a straight question:

'I wish you would be so good as to give me your opinion, in the best manner you can, one way or the other, whether, upon the whole you have heard of the symptoms described, it is your opinion the death proceeded from that medicine or any other cause.'

But Mr Hunter, deeply conscious of his wretchedly inadequate performance, could only reply, 'That question is distressing. I do not mean to equivocate, but when I tell the sentiments of my own mind, what I feel at the time, I can give nothing decisive.'

And on this totally unsatisfactory note, the witness was allowed to stand down, only too aware that the Defence's big gun had been transformed into the dampest of damp squibs. He was in fact much chastened by the experience, and subsequently in his public lectures expressed regret that before his appearance at the trial he had not made a closer study of the effects of poisons on human beings.

With the evidence on both sides concluded, Mr Justice Buller began his summing-up by instructing the jury to 'strip your minds' of any 'false and cruel reports' that might have been circulated in the public prints. You will, he urged, 'take nothing into your consideration that has not been proved in the course of the trial.'

He then returned to the point he had made at the beginning of the Assize: all of the evidence put forward by the Prosecution was, inevitably, circumstantial. However, far from being a weakness, 'if the circumstances are such, as when laid together bring conviction to your minds, it is then fully equal, if not, as I told you before, more convincing than positive evidence.' This, as was noted earlier, was a radical departure from established practice and one that was to be hotly disputed by other lawyers.

Having summarised the evidence, he told the jury that they had first to ask themselves: did the deceased die of poison? The Crown had called 'a great number of very able men in the physical line', all of whom had no doubt that this was the case.

The Defence, on the other hand, had presented just one gentleman 'who is likewise of the faculty, and a very able man.' Intentionally or otherwise, the judge thus neatly put Mr Hunter on a par with the local physicians, drawing no comparison between the former's vast experience and international standing and Dr Rattray's admission that he had never carried out a single human autopsy. He also failed to point out that although the Prosecution had called Mr Bucknill, he had not been asked a single question on the operation even though it was he who had performed it.

Similarly, the judge ignored completely Hunter's opinion of the inadequacy of the autopsy, where the failure to investigate the body thoroughly was the reason for his doubts over the cause of death. On the other hand, his honest admission of these doubts, which contrasted so markedly with the firm conviction of the Prosecution's witnesses, came in for scathing criticism.

'I can hardly say what his opinion is,' declared His Lordship, 'for he does not seem to have formed any opinion at all of the matter... I wished very much to have got a direct answer from Mr Hunter, if I could, what, upon the whole was now the result of his attention and application to the subject, and what was his present opinion, but he says he can say nothing decisive. So that, upon this point, if you are to determine upon the evidence of the gentlemen who are skilled in the faculty only, you have the *very positive* opinion of four or five gentlemen of the faculty that the deceased did die of poison. On the other side, you have what I really cannot myself call more than the *doubt* of the other.'

He then turned to the testimony of Lady Boughton and once again, despite his stern injunction to the jury to clear their minds of all prejudicial emotions, his exposition was far from impartial. Suppressing his private opinion that the woman was a fool whose word could not be relied on, he treated as indisputable her evidence of, for instance, the accused's rinsing of the medicine phials. He clearly regarded this episode as crucial and came back to it as he neared the end of his summing-up: 'That circumstance (to which I can find no answer whatever) of his rinsing out the bottle does carry strong marks of knowledge in him, that there was something in that bottle which he wished should never be discovered.'

This makes it all the more unfortunate that he did not draw the jury's attention to the fact that Lady Boughton's version of these events differed extensively from her evidence at the Inquest, as had been clearly demonstrated by the Defence in its cross-examination. In fact, whenever any conflict arose between her testimony and the claims of the accused, he consistently dismissed the latter as fabrications. For example, Donellan had asserted that when the deceased returned from fishing his stockings were wet. 'Lady Boughton has proved to you that they were not wet, and that they had not the appearance of having been so. This is therefore another falsehood. The prisoner, in a letter addressed to the Coroner and his jury, says that it was the established rule, and had been for months in Lady Boughton's family, to eat nothing out of the same dish with Sir Theodosius. Lady Boughton swears that she knew of no such rule, but that they daily eat out of the same dish, and drank out of the same cup with him. This assertion is, of course, another falsehood.'

It was not only Lady Boughton's evidence that he treated in this way. Turning to the highly suspect story told by Francis Amos, the gardener, of Donellan's boasting to him that he was 'master now', he commented, 'Here you have a voluntary acknowledgement of the true nature of the prisoner's wishes. He wanted to be master!'

Similarly, although he had had personal experience of that shifty bankrupt, John Darbyshire, he made no attempt to advise the jury to consider carefully the reliability of his account of the conversations in the prison cell where, according to him, the accused made a series of allegations implicating others in Sir Theodosius's death. 'What,' demanded His Lordship, 'is to be collected from these strange incompatible, unmeaning falsehoods? If these kind of contradictory declarations prove nothing else, they at least prove this, that there must have been sinister intentions in the author of them, for no man involves himself in systematic falsehood for nothing.'

He did concede that the incident of Donellan's trying to establish an alibi in his questioning of the coachman was, in all the circumstances, understandable. However, his words and actions during the failed attempts to open the body were, in the judge's opinion, much more suspicious. He had, it was true, in his letters to Sir William Wheler expressed an urgent desire for this to take place and for Sir William to be present, 'but the question for you to consider is whether, upon the whole of his conduct, he did endeavour to have the body opened but has repeatedly prevented it, that will be much stronger than his saying once, twice or twenty times that he wished it.'

With regard to the missed opportunity of Mr Bucknill and Mr Snow, His Lordship censured the Defence for its failure to call the latter on the prisoner's behalf 'to prove what passed between them, and what information he gave to Mr Snow.' Surely though the same criticism could have been levelled at the Prosecution for they too, one would have thought, would have wanted to establish just why Snow left before his colleague's return and what his parting instructions (which Donellan claimed were to proceed with the burial at once) had actually been.

In fact, whenever there were two ways to look at the evidence the judge almost invariably came down on the side of the Crown. Dealing with the deceased's being rescued from various 'scrapes', he gave Donellan some credit for this but then reminded the jury that all the incidents took place 'at a distance in time before the death of Sir Theodosius.'

He also commented on the fact that no evidence had been produced to support the accused's assertion that on his marriage he had renounced all claim to his wife's property. The thought might have occurred to him that in his own case he had certainly not acted in such a self-sacrificial manner. After all, what motive could there possibly be for elopement other than personal enrichment? But he would not, of course, give voice to such an idea.

Whatever impact this highly prejudiced review had on the jury, not all those present in court were impressed. The representative of the *Lloyds Evening Post* commented acidly, 'The judge convinced his auditors that the powers of consummate reasoning were not the most splendid talents in his valuable character, but that his humanity bore entire pace with his other endowments.'

In conclusion, His Lordship returned to the nature of the evidence on which the entire case was based. 'You must take all the circumstances of the case together into your consideration, and remember that it is for you to form your own opinions and to decide upon the fate of the prisoner, in the doing of which I am sure you will act according to the best of your judgement and your conscience to find out the truth of the case, and as you find that truth, so you will pronounce your verdict.'

And so, at last, the jury retired to begin their deliberations. As he watched them withdraw, Donellan, on the surface at least, maintained the air of confidence he had exuded throughout the trial. According to the account in the *Coventry Mercury*, 'he turned to a gentleman he had formerly known and asked him what his opinion of the evidence was, and what verdict he thought the jury would return.'

Certainly, if they were willing to set aside the judge's own views, there was much for them to consider: the conflicting medical evidence and the various possible explanations for the deceased's death, the accused's claim that he did not stand to benefit from that death, the inconsistencies in Lady Boughton's testimony, the absence of any proof of his ever having distilled laurel water, and many other areas of dispute. But the time was now twenty-five minutes past six, eleven long hours since the trial had begun and, with the end of their week's obligations in sight at last, the members of the jury had homes to go to, businesses to attend to, lives that had been put on hold to take up once more.

And so, after just nine minutes of no doubt earnest consideration and intense debate, they returned to pronounce the only possible verdict: Guilty.

Chapter Fourteen

**'The hungry judges soon the sentence sign,
And wretches hang that jurymen may dine.'**

TO A man more given to self-awareness than Mr Justice Buller, Alexander Pope's lines from *The Rape of the Lock* might have struck a chord as he prepared to embark on his final duty of the day. The black cap having been taken down and placed on his head, he addressed himself directly to the prisoner: 'John Donellan, you now stand convicted, on the clearest evidence that could be produced, of the crime of murder, which of all crimes, next to those against the state, the government or the constitution, is the most atrocious. Of all murders, poisoning is the most horrible; and if there may be degrees allowed in that species of guilt, that of which you are now convicted surpasses all others of the kind that went before yours, as much as murder itself surpasses other crimes.'

The relationship with the deceased, the betrayal of trust, the motive, the premeditated nature of the crime – all served only to increase its heinous nature. Returning once more to the nature of the evidence (almost as though he was himself conscious of the dubious nature of the weight he attached to it), he went on, 'In your case there appears to be a peculiar interference of heaven to bring the crime to light; for out of the very extraordinary pains which you took to conceal the offence, circumstances have arisen that are so singular in their nature, and so correspondent with each other, that they have indubitably marked you as the perpetrator of this murder. In a fact of so secret a kind, circumstantial evidence is the only evidence that can generally be expected; and in your case, circumstances have appeared, than which, I will venture to say, no stronger have ever been known.'

Then, after the customary exhortation that 'during the short time you have now to live, a deep contrition for your manifold sins is the only means you have left to make your peace hereafter', he solemnly pronounced the sentence of the law: 'that you, John Donellan, be taken from hence to the place from whence you came, and on Monday next, that you be carried to the place of execution, there to be hanged by the neck until you are dead; and that your body be afterwards given to the surgeons to be dissected and anatomised; and the Lord have mercy on your soul.'

The *Lloyds Evening Post* reporter was impressed by Donellan's reaction. 'The prisoner bore this solemn and fatal decree with an extraordinary fortitude, and did not, in any part of his conduct, during the trying situation of the day, display appearances like either temerity or cowardice, but demeaned himself with a decent moderation, that must have excited universal sympathy in any case less eminently horrid than his own.'

The *Coventry Mercury* saw things slightly differently: 'During the whole of the trial, which lasted nearly twelve hours, the prisoner stood to all appearance totally resigned to his fate, but the judge's speech at passing sentence manifestly very much affected him.'

Whatever the truth, there was of course a deep irony behind the fate awaiting Donellan's corpse, with dissection and anatomising playing such a crucial role in the case. It would take place at the Town Hall (now the County Museum) in the nearby Market Square. But when, on completion of the sentence, the jailer, in time-honoured fashion, urged him to 'turn to the judge and beg your body off from dissection', Donellan merely shrugged, declaring, 'It is perfectly indifferent to me what becomes of my body.'

Most of the public prints extended their coverage of the trial with eye-witness accounts of Donellan's demeanour during his final days. On 9th April the *Coventry Mercury* carried the following 'Particulars respecting the behaviour and execution of the unfortunate Captain Donellan, who was executed on Monday last, at Warwick.'

The account began with the Friday evening: 'Immediately after the conviction of Captain Donellan, a divine, accompanied by a particular friend of the prisoner, went to see him, and to all appearance he was perfectly resigned to his unhappy fate. It was urged to him that as the evidence had been so clear, a denial of the fact would be looked upon by the world as a means of prevarication, and would induce people to throw additional insult upon his memory. To this observation he answered, he could not help any man's conclusions, he knew his own heart, and would with his last breath assert his innocence. Some few unguarded and unpremeditated expressions, aggravated by falsehoods of the most flagrant kind, which were sworn at his trial, had induced a jury to take his life, but time would do him justice, and prove him an injured man, ruined by those who ought to have been his friends.

'Perceiving the gentlemen in astonishment at this conversation, he added that he should dedicate tomorrow to the purpose of drawing up an answer to, and a refutation of, the evidence, and should leave it with a friend, that he had no doubt would comply with the last request he should make, that of seeing it correctly published. He was asked whether he had not a desire to see his wife, and take a last farewell. To this he hastily replied, I do beseech you let me not hear again of this; if she does not come I shall die composed.

'On Sunday evening he deposited his case with a gentleman of Coventry, who assisted him in his trial, with an earnest request that he would print and publish it. He then gave some directions relative to the adjustment of the said operation, which was to take place in the morning, and appeared remarkably cheerful and composed.'

This though did not prevent him from writing one last letter to Theodosia which vividly conveys the depth of his bitterness at what he saw as her frailty and her mother's treachery:

My once esteemed Wife,

Do not think that I am about to reproach you for declining your visits to me in my present ignominious situation; I am better satisfied that you did not even attempt it. Brought together by the hand of indifference, it would be a mockery of feeling to affect a concern for our separation, disgraceful as it is about to prove. To argue with you on the score of those dark arts which have undone me, would be fruitless; because I know your *conjugal* has ever been subservient to your *filial* affection. As to your – mother – but I will suppress my indignation; if however you should wish to know my dying sentiments of her, ask our friend W-son, the mournful bearer of this, and he will not hesitate to impart them to you, because I shall charge him with my last breath not to refuse you such a request. Were I to advise your immediate separation from her, it would have no weight; for my little influence over you has long been at an end! Mrs H-, you well know, has for a series of years treated me with a tender and disinterested regard; let it not surprise you then to learn, that I have bequeathed her my gold watch and miniature picture, as the last and strongest token I can give her of my gratitude. As to our two poor children, if you deem them pledges of our love, cherish them as such, but try to conceal from them their father's unhappy fate. I have been long combating unnumbered wishes that pressed me to clasp them in my fond arms, and bid them a last adieu! Thank God, however, I have at length subdued them: the whole world, except my own offspring, are welcome to become the spectators of my ignominious, though unmerited exit!

If I have omitted any thing that I should have said to you – your own heart, I trust, will urge it for me, when I shall be no more: – Farewell.

John Donellan

Warwick Gaol, Sunday night, April 1, 1781

At seven o'clock on the Monday morning, as Donellan was being taken the half mile out of town on the Heathcote road to Gallows Hill, two of his fellow accused at the Assize were also spending their final moments in this life. John Hammond and Thomas Pitmore, condemned for the murder of the butcher, Wilfred Berwick, were to be hanged at Washwood Heath, near their native Birmingham. Although they were by that stage past caring, the fate awaiting their bodies was if anything worse than that of Donellan's, for they were to remain hanging in chains until the flesh rotted from their bones.

But this was a mere sideshow compared with the spectacle that was so eagerly awaited in Warwick. The crowd lining the route and, even more, pressed around the gallows, did not have long to wait before Donellan, 'dressed in a suit of deep mourning ... was carried to the place of execution in a mourning coach, followed by a hearse, and the Sheriff's officers in deep mourning; as he went on, he frequently put his head out of the coach and earnestly desired the prayers of the people around him.' On his arrival at the platform, he alighted from the coach and ascended the ladder to the platform, where the hangman apologised to him for the early hour, explaining that he would also be carrying out the other two executions.

The anonymous eye-witness continues that, having 'prayed for a considerable time, and joined in the usual service with the greatest appearance of devotion; he then in an audible tone of voice addressed the spectators in the following terms: That as he was then going to appear before God, to whom all deceit was known, he solemnly declared *that he was innocent of the crime for which he was to suffer*! That he had drawn up a vindication of himself, which he hoped the world would believe, for it was of more consequence to him to speak truth than falsehood, and had no doubt but that time would reveal the many mysteries that had arisen in his trial, and prove that he fell a sacrifice to the malice and black designs of his —.' This was presumably one final barb levelled at Lady Boughton, but the publications, wisely in view of the law of libel, deleted it.

Finally, 'after praying fervently some time, he let his handkerchief fall, a signal agreed on between him and the executioner, and was launched into eternity.'

Chapter Fifteen

THE PUBLIC'S fascination with the case, far from dying along with the supposed perpetrator, only increased, with rumours and illfounded gossip continuing unabated. Had not Donellan's own solicitor, on the very morning after the trial, and newly come from a visit to the condemned man, been overheard, in the public room at the Three Tuns Inn in Warwick, admit that he was fully convinced of his client's guilt? And did he not also say that the villain had declared bitterly that a greater piece of work was made about killing one man in England than twenty in Ireland?

And while it had to be acknowledged that no evidence had been produced at the trial of his distilling laurel leaves, was it not true that the blackguard had privately confessed to their use, with the ridiculous assertion that this was to relieve the gout from which he claimed to suffer? And, moreover, in his distilling chamber was there not found a copy of Dr Mortimer's *Philosophical Transactions*, with the leaf turned down at the very account of the poisonous effects of laurel water on the human body? And were these facts, well known to his own lawyers, not disclosed, as was their duty, to the Crown?

The coverage also continued in the public prints, with detailed accounts of the trial appearing by the very next day. Following the descriptions of the execution, some readers were sufficiently impressed by his demeanour and affirmation of his innocence to doubt the rightness of the verdict. To others though these were just the final signs of his depravity. An anonymous correspondent to the *Coventry Mercury* put this view forcibly:

'To argue from the dying declaration of Captain Donellan that he was not guilty is the highest offence to truth and the grossest perversion of reason. People will say, of what service could it be, on his just launching into eternity, to deny the murder? I will tell them, he denied the fact which his ambition made him commit, as a revenge on those by whose testimony the views of that ambition were frustrated … His religious exhortations were hypocrisy, to cover his intended declaration of innocence; and his absence of fear at the moment of death is only to be ascribed to his disbelief of the omnipotence of a Deity. He must either have been the most virtuous, the most religious, and the most injured man alive, or he was the veriest villain that ever enjoyed the light of reason. In his case there is no medium.'

Meanwhile, the two shorthand writers, Blanchard and Gurney, were engaged in a hectic race to be the first to reach the booksellers. The result was, in fact, a virtual dead heat, with both accounts being published within two weeks of the trial.

Each, of course, laid claim to being the only authentic version and cautioning the public, as the advertisement for Blanchard's version put it, 'not to be imposed on by various spurious editions which are now circulating, none being genuine except the above, which will be published in a few days, in folio, and may be bound up with the state trials.'

Then, on April 23rd, another advertisement appeared: 'This day is published, in folio, to bind with the state trials, price 2s 6d, The Case of John Donellan, Esq. As read over and approved by him after his conviction for the murder of Sir Theodosius Boughton. London: Printed for John Bell, British Library, Strand.' Even before this 'authorised version' appeared, much of its content had formed the lead story in successive issues of the *Lloyds Evening Post* of April 16th and 18th (at the bargain price of three pence each), in much the same way as best sellers are serialised in the press today ahead of their publication in book form.

With nothing to distract him, not even a final visit from his wife, Donellan had devoted the last two days of his life to its composition. The published version, costing three shillings, had the revised title of *A Defence and Substance of the Trial of John Donellan Esquire… Founded on the Case solemnly attested by the Sufferer after his Conviction, and published at the Request of his Solicitors, Messrs Inge and Webb*. It is prefaced by a declaration, dated Sunday, April 1, 1781, witnessed by William Rowe, Jun. – possibly the Warwick gaoler, although elsewhere the name is spelt Roe – and Richard Reynolds, and signed John Donellan: 'This case has been read over to me this day, being the last day of my life; and it contains nothing but real facts, as far as my knowledge goes, and I solemnly request and firmly desire that it may be published, as a firm vindication of my honour and character, to the World. I also desire that Mr. Webb, one of my Solicitors, may be the whole and sole publisher of it, as a clear testimony of my being perfectly satisfied with his conduct.'

Thomas Webb had been true to his word and ensured its publication – despite the fact that it contained serious criticisms of the conduct of the Defence. Acutely conscious of the increasingly widespread view of its inadequacy, Mr Webb and his fellow solicitor, Edward Inge, headed the text with an 'Address' to the reader:

> 'Since the trial it has been universally believed, with how much justice is not for us to decide, that the defence for the unfortunate sufferer on the trial was a very imperfect one; and that his conviction was chiefly imputable to the neglect of his lawyers.' They were accused of being 'very inattentive' and failing to make 'proper suggestions' to their counsel, but it was for the latter to judge whether their proposals 'were pertinent or not' and it was they who 'adjudged as much as was necessary.'

It is likely that much of the content had been prepared by Donellan ahead of the trial and presented to his lawyers to help them prepare his defence. Certainly, it is of considerable length, running to forty-six folio pages and well over thirty seven thousand words, whereas the 'Prisoner's Defence' that was read to the court was a mere fourteen hundred words long.

The first section, following his instructions, was in fact contributed by the solicitors and consists of a detailed account of the depositions given at the Coroner's Inquest, 'particularly that of Lady Boughton, pointing out the various inconsistencies and direct contradictions which appeared in her testimony then delivered, compared with that which was ultimately given before the Judge on the trial.'

The *Defence* itself is written in the third person and begins with a brief account of Donellan's life up to his marriage. This is, as one might expect, highly selective, with no mention of his illegitimacy or ignominious dismissal from the East India Company. We are merely told that, 'On his return to England, he was put upon half pay in the 39th Regiment of Foot, on producing a certificate of his good behaviour to the then Secretary of State of War, Lord Barrington, and is now in receipt of the same.'

No mention is made either of his position at the Pantheon or the elopement with Theodosia, merely that 'in June 1777 he intermarried with Miss Boughton.' He repeats the assertion made in his trial statement that on his marriage he renounced all claim to his wife's fortune, both what she then owned and might possess in the future. At this time he also made his will, under which Theodosius would inherit his sister's property should she die before him and without issue. He provided his Defence team with details of the attorney who executed this – a Mr White of Castle Yard, Holborn – but even though his desire to get hold of Theodosius's money was seen as the prime motive for the alleged murder his Counsel chose not to follow this up, leaving the way clear for the judge in his summing-up to comment acidly on the absence of any evidence to back up his claim.

Summarising the situation within the Boughton family, Donellan takes the first of several sideswipes at Lady Boughton, whom he clearly felt was the most to blame for his downfall. Having sent her son to Eton, she gave him only a niggardly allowance for 'pocket money', eighteen pence a week, rising eventually to half a crown, 'so that Sir Theodosius finding the same far unequal to the expenses he was necessarily put unto, was obliged to think of some other means of procuring money, and being young and unexperienced, had recourse to Jews, as Mr Donellan was informed by him. By this mode of supply it is, however, natural to suppose that he was furnished with plenty of money, and if that can be believed, it is equally reasonable to suppose that the same tempted him to enter into debaucheries and follies which he might not perhaps have thought of, had his mother made him an allowance suitable to his birth and fortune.'

The account continues with Theodosius's removal from Eton, Lady Boughton's letters to Donellan and her daughter expressing her concern over his 'complaint', her 'several pressing invitations to Lawford Hall', which were finally accepted, and Theodosius's confession to Donellan that he was 'quacking himself' with, amongst other remedies, 'mercurial ointment'. During the trial, both Mr Powell and Lady Boughton had tried to underplay their concerns over his health and, as was noted earlier, the latter had, at Donellan's instigation, been instructed to present to the court both the bills from the various surgeons she had employed and the memorandum found in her son's bedroom after his death detailing where and when he had contracted his '*last*' infection' and the effects of the medicines that the apothecary had prescribed. However, as Donellan notes bitterly, his Defence Counsel 'did not think it prudent or necessary' to ask for these and 'therefore the Court remained ignorant of Sir Theodosius's having ever had any other Venereal

Complaint than the last Infection, or of his ever having taken or used Mercury at all.'

He then gives his version of how he spent the evening before Theodosius's death, commenting on Lady Boughton's 'strange story' that he had told her he had been fishing with her son: 'Indeed the whole story seems improbable; for it would have been absurd to the last Degree in Mr Donellan to have said that … when he knew the Gardeners and others could so flatly contradict it.' He also registers his regret that Mr Newnham decided against calling Messrs Dand and Matthew to support his claim that he had spent a considerable amount of time with them, even though this would have further undermined Lady Boughton's credibility.

After telling how he and Theodosia left the parlour and retired to bed, he gives a detailed description of the layout of the Hall:

'The room Mr and Mrs Donellan slept in was directly over the parlour before mentioned, and the staircase leading to it adjoins the said parlour door, so that he was up in his room in less than a minute, and must be heard there by Lady Boughton in less than that time; from whence he did not stir till morning.

'The staircase before mentioned leads to Mr and Mrs Donellan's room, and another room or two … and to those rooms only, and the same rooms have no kind of communication with any other part of the house. Sir Theodosius's room was quite on the other side of the house; therefore if Mr Donellan had visited his room before he went to bed he must have first returned down the before-mentioned staircase (which he could not have done without being observed by Lady Boughton, the parlour door being open the whole of the evening) and then have went through the house upwards of eighty yards, and up the distant staircase; a matter impracticable without being seen by some of the servants. But even supposing Mr Donellan could have had access to Sir Theodosius's room, unobserved, as it was then dark it would have been nearly impossible for him to have distinguished any particular bottle from the various number then in the room.

'Thus, the impossibility of Mr Donellan having access to Sir Theodosius's room, from the time of the medicine being delivered to him by Samuel Frost to the time of his death is obvious, unless we could imagine that he went into the room the morning of his death, and mixed poison in the medicine while Sir Theodosius was in bed, the idea of which is too absurd to be mentioned.'

This line of reasoning carries considerable weight, making it all the more regrettable that once again the Defence completely ignored the chance to, at the very least, sow seeds of doubt in the minds of the jury.

Moving on to the next morning, after narrating how he came to ride alone to Newnham Wells and the panic that greeted his return, Donellan describes the scene in Theodosius's bedroom, where he found the youth 'in the agonies of death… He looked upon the sad spectacle with horror and amazement for some little time, and then Sir Theodosius went off; upon which, he turned to Lady Boughton, and in a tone of voice which evidently marked his being affected at this melancholy event, asked her what she had given her son, and where the bottle was which contained the physic.'

Methinks the Captain doth protest too much, perhaps, but he was having to confront here what was, according to Mr Justice Buller, the most compelling of all the circumstances proving his guilt – the supposed rinsing of the bottles. Whilst pointing out the contradictions in Lady Boughton's accounts, he gives his own version of the episode: that he had merely put 'about a teaspoonful of water' into the phial, poured this into a small basin and dipped his finger in it in order to taste it.

He argues that 'if he had wished thereby to have cleaned the bottle, a larger quantity of water would most certainly have effected it better than so small a quantity as a teaspoonful. The fact was that he knew a large quantity would drown what little of the medicine might remain on the sides of the phial, if any, and that therefore the smaller the quantity he put in, the more likely he would be to taste what the medicine was.' In any case, if he had wanted to remove all trace of the bottle's contents 'he would have done it more secretly, and not before Lady Boughton and Sarah Blundell.'

As far as clearing the room was concerned, he claims that it was Lady Boughton who began this, probably because some of the other phials and gallipots on the mantelpiece and, in particular, the close stool 'smelt very offensively.' He therefore told the maid to help her mistress and 'happening at the time she was taking away the things to stand near the chimney piece, where the chief part of the bottles stood, and seeing Sarah Blundell coming up to take them away, put some of them into her apron, which was all the assistance he gave, and which was nothing more than anyone else might have very innocently done.'

If, he continued, he had intended to destroy all evidence of what the supposedly fatal bottle contained he would either have told the maid to throw away all the phials or watched where she took them in order to remove them himself. It was only nine or ten days later, when Mr Caldecott, the solicitor employed by the Prosecution, enquired after it that he learned that she had 'put them into a hole in the kitchen, sometimes used for stewing.' He retrieved what he thought was the bottle in question, showed it to Samuel Frost, who had brought the potion from Mr Powell, to confirm this then took it 'into the parlour and put it upon the harpsichord, ready to be produced when required.'

Moving on to the correspondence with Sir William Wheler, Donellan gives an accurate summary of their contents, which were of course disclosed at the trial, but is on much shakier ground when describing the visit of Dr Rattray and Mr Wilmer. He says that he gave them the letters, the clear implication being that these included the one where rumours of poison were mentioned. He also, he says, told them that it was the wish, both of Sir William and the family, 'that the body of Sir Theodosius should be opened to discover, if possible, the cause of his death.' This is correct as far as it goes but again he avoided all suggestion that the 'cause' might be poison.

His recollection of the conversation following the doctors' decision not to proceed with the autopsy is at variance with Rattray's version. He asserts that he 'expressed a wish that Sir William Wheler should know the result of their attendance; and in order that he might have the greater satisfaction, requested Dr Rattray to wait upon him the next day, who replied that he should see Sir William, he believed, the next day and would then inform him what had been done.'

Rattray, on the other hand, said under cross-examination at the trial that, as far as he could recall, he had replied that he did not think he would be able to as he already had a pressing engagement for the following day. Wilmer, though, agreed with Donellan's account, testifying that his colleague had said 'he believed he should, and would give him an account of the business.'

Both at the Inquest, when he readily admitted that the body was in such a state of putrefaction that he could not express an opinion on the cause of death, and during the trial itself, Wilmer came across as being far less hostile to the accused than his colleague, and for this he won Donellan's approbation:

> 'Mr Wilmer's conduct in this business has been as contrary to Dr
> Rattray's as possible. He has observed the strictest impartiality and

has ever been consistent, as well in what he said before the Coroner as in his behaviour and conversation since. He is a man of the first eminence in his profession of a surgeon in Warwickshire; and his character as a gentleman and a man of humane disposition is universally known.'

Rattray, on the other hand, was the object of Donellan's particular anger. It is clear, he asserts, that he was determined to give 'as unfavourable account of this business as he can; but whether, from his being very much connected with Sir William Wheler, and from hopes thereby of pleasing him, or from a wish which he may have to gain popularity, by setting up his opinion in contradiction to every other gentleman of the faculty (which he did at one time) or from what other motive, is not known.' Furthermore, he played a leading role in 'the management and direction of the Prosecution against Mr Donellan.' The brief was shown to him as soon as it was drawn up, for his approval, and 'he has, in many companies, even went so far as to say, "We shall subpoena such a person; and we shall do this and do that", which are strong proofs of the part he has taken.'

Whilst allowing for Donellan's understandable bias, this would go a long way to explaining why at the trial, of all the physicians, Rattray was given the greatest prominence by the Prosecution, even though it was his faulty diagnosis that led to the attribution of arsenic as the cause of death and the fact that he had not personally carried out the autopsy.

The other medical man to come under fire was Mr Powell. Whilst admitting condescendingly that he is 'in general, considered as a well-meaning man', Donellan declares that 'his conduct in this business has certainly been very extraordinary.' On the morning of Sir Theodosius's death 'it undoubtedly would have been natural' for anyone in Mr Powell's position, especially as at that time his own potions were considered the most likely cause of the fatality, to have examined his patient and tried to resuscitate him.

'But instead of attempting to bleed Sir Theodosius or to take any steps to recover him, Mr Powell only took his hand, and putting it down again, said, "He is dead", and then went out of the room, and did not ask a single question, but wishing Mr Donellan and Lady Boughton a good morning, went away; the whole time of his being there not exceeding ten minutes.'

Theodosius had been dead for well over an hour by the time the apothecary arrived so this criticism is not entirely fair. But Donellan was perhaps influenced by the fact that at the trial Powell had insisted that his patient's state of health was essentially sound, whereas, at least according to Donellan, he on several occasions expressed his concern about the youth's treating himself with mercury. However, in his very brief cross-examination, Mr Newnham did not raise this or question him about a letter, dated June 13th, in which he asked Donellan 'please to inform Sir Theodosius Boughton that I mean he should take the bolus over night, the purge the next morning, and the apozem the same morning.'

This is surely another instance of the casual approach of the Defence, for it clearly shows that Powell had been treating the young man for longer than the two months he stated in his evidence, both at the Inquest and the trial, and that he was prescribing more varied treatments than the simple 'cooling physick' he claimed to be giving.

Donellan also asserts that the apothecary left the first session of the Inquest at the same time as Lady Boughton and himself and as they were about to mount their horses to return home, he remarked that 'he was as glad as though anybody had given him fifty pounds that Sir Theodosius had been opened, and that he was present, for that nothing was more free from poison.' His opinion would have been less likely to impress the jury than that of the doctors present at the autopsy – although at that stage, none of them, not even Rattray, was prepared to go so far as mention poison – but even so he could have been questioned on this during cross-examination.

On the subject of the autopsy, Donellan states that Mr Bucknill preserved the fluid that was taken from the stomach and gave it to a dog, but it 'only made him a little sick, and had no worse effect.' If this really was the case, it was another serious lapse on the part of Defence Counsel not to question Bucknill on this, for it would have gone some way to countering the evidence of the various experiments on animals conducted by the medical witnesses.

Donellan though goes further, alleging that his 'adversaries' had tried to keep this incident 'an entire secret', and this was part and parcel of the unscrupulous manner in which the case against him had been built up. He claims that undue pressure was brought on vulnerable individuals, particularly the Hall servants. 'Several gentlemen, in the neighbourhood of Lawford Hall, have at different times sent for the witnesses against Mr Donellan to their respective houses and extorted many things from them which were intended to be adduced at the trial. They have even went so far as to threaten them with imprisonment and other punishments and, calling in their clerks, several times have given them absolute orders to make out commitments, if they did not say something more against Mr Donellan.'

He cites the evidence of Francis Amos, who told the story of his boasting that he was now master of the Hall. According to Donellan, what actually happened was that the gardener asked him who, following the death of Sir Theodosius, was the owner and he replied, correctly, that it now belonged to the heir, Sir Edward Boughton. This is a far more likely scenario and, as Donellan points out, Amos was questioned closely by the Coroner at the Inquest but 'as it appearing that he knew nothing either for or against Mr Donellan, his name was not mentioned in the depositions.' However, between then and the trial, 'the poor fellow being a weak, silly, illiterate man, and having been threatened with punishment, matters were extorted from him which he knew nothing of, and which were entirely false and groundless.'

Even more ruthless was the treatment of Sarah Blundell. She, as the maid who was present during the alleged bottle rinsing and clearing of Theodosius's room, was potentially a key witness for the Crown. She, of course, died in childbirth before the trial, but even on her deathbed the pressure was unrelenting:

'During the time this woman was in labour she was so extremely ill that it was expected she would die before a delivery; and as Mrs Donellan was particularly humane to her she told her, in the presence of Sukey Sparrow, Mrs Donellan's maid, that she knew no harm of her husband, and that she told Mr B-, every time he sent for her, she knew nothing against him. This was spoke at a time when she thought of dying every moment.'

Although the girl had backed up her mistress at the Inquest, Lady Boughton was not one to forgive this, as she saw it, disloyalty, and despite her condition she was sent packing, carried from the Hall on a cart. Even then though, she was not left in peace. 'She lingered upwards of a fortnight afterwards; and during that time every unfair advantage was taken to extort things from her, and Mr Caldecott, the solicitor in this prosecution, was with her the day of her death, but she was speechless that day, and the day preceding.'

The Defence, of course, had engaged in their own share of 'dirty tricks' by failing to disclose to the Prosecution the fact that their client had distilled laurel leaves, which by the legal requirement of 'discovery' they should have done. In his *Defence* Donellan admits that he had used them but claims that this was 'along with other ingredients for preparing an aromatic bath for his feet, which he constantly used after a fit of the gout, and found it to be very strengthening and serviceable.'

To the more cynically inclined, this is reminiscent of Madeline Smith, accused of poisoning her lover and whose trial in 1857 resulted in the Scottish verdict of 'Not Proven', and Florence Maybrick, convicted forty years later of the murder of her husband, both of whom explained their purchase of large quantities of arsenic as being for cosmetic purposes. Donellan, however, claimed that he had recommended the treatment to Lady Boughton and also told his lawyers the title of the book where he had found the concoction, *The Toilet of Flora* (not the rumoured *Philososphical Transactions*), which had been published in 1779. But they clearly thought it wiser not to draw the Crown's attention to this potentially tricky point.

The *Defence* also includes Mr Justice Buller's initial Charge to the Jury and his summing up, and, despite his lack of legal training, Donellan puts his finger on the two elements that were to provoke particular criticism from many of the judge's fellow lawyers. He argues against Buller's contention that circumstantial evidence can provide as valuable evidence as undisputed fact, declaring that the former 'I will be bold to assert can, at best, no more compare with positive than conjecture with certainty.'

He also states that the judge was wrong to dismiss John Hunter's evidence so scornfully. Any doubts that he admitted about the cause of death were due to the failings of the autopsy, and in any case in his evidence-in-chief his opinion had been 'full as positive' as any offered by the witnesses for the Crown. 'It is astonishing,' Donellan declares, 'to find the learned judge stating in his comments on the evidence that Mr Hunter had only given his doubt in opposition to the positive testimony of the others... Is it doubt to state that apoplexy would produce all the symptoms' or that the appearance of the body after death 'arose entirely from putrefaction?'

The volume also contains an account of Donellan's execution, even more sympathetically inclined than the earlier reports – so much so that one wonders if it was written by Donellan himself, putting a favourable gloss on his actions to the very last. 'He died a Christian in every respect; yet uniformly, solemnly, and eagerly protested his innocence to the last.'

And here of course lies the final irony. Even allowing for the inevitable special pleading, there are one feels sufficient elements in the *Defence* to give one pause. At the very least, they substantiate Donellan's assertion that he was ill-served by his Counsel. But however persuasive the document might be, it was of course an academic exercise, for within hours of its completion its author was dead.

Chapter Sixteen

THE PUBLICATION of Donellan's personal testimony gave renewed impetus to the controversy that the trial had aroused, with the debate continuing well into the twentieth century. Whilst some found his arguments persuasive, others were less impressed. William Roughead, writing in the *Juridical Review* of June 1922, declared that the document 'may best be defined as length without breadth. Plausible and ingenious, as a piece of special pleading it does no discredit to the ability of the composer; but regarded as a refutation of the sworn facts, it leaves much to be desired.'

It is certainly true that its tone bears a marked resemblance to Donellan's earlier *Case*, addressed to the Court of Directors of the East India Company, in which he makes similarly eloquent but largely uncorroborated claims about his impeccable behaviour, which has been so sadly, and in the latter instance tragically, misunderstood. However, leaving aside his contribution and concentrating solely on the evidence given at the trial and Mr Justice Buller's handling of it, many commentators were far from convinced that justice had been done, let alone seen to be done.

Within weeks of the trial there appeared a sixty-page tract, *The Case of John Donellan, Esquire, impartially considered, abstractedly from the man or crime; but only as to the Law*, by A Lawyer. The key word is 'impartially' for the writer argues forcibly that the judge was far from impartial in his conduct of the trial. Drawing extensively on established legal precedent and practice, he argues that he failed in his duty to 'help the offender, according to truth, as far as reason and justice may allow.' It is, he declares, 'a maxim of the Laws of England that a judge can know nothing as a judge but what he knows judicially.'

The author was apparently unaware that, before the trial had even begun, Buller had been heard to say that the accused was clearly guilty, but his contention that 'the evidence in a court of justice must be legal, that is, such as convinces Mr Justice Buller, and not merely Francis Buller, esquire' is particularly apposite.

Whilst acknowledging that, with all the preceding adverse publicity, a Warwickshire jury was likely to be prejudiced against the prisoner (despite the judge's rightful admonition to ignore this) the fact that they reached their verdict in such an astonishingly short time suggests that they were 'liable to be hurried away by their opinion of the integrity, eloquence and abilities of the judge.'

For 'A Lawyer', the first and third qualities were, in this case at least, scandalously absent. The initial charge to the Grand Jury showed, in his view, a blatant bias. Two-thirds of the charge were devoted to a series of hypothetical situations: murder by proxy, with the guilty individual ensuring that poison is given to the victim without himself being present, the substitution of a harmless medicine with a noxious substance, and the irrelevance of the erroneous identification of the poison used. Of all the cases the jury would be hearing in the coming week, these would apply only to Donellan's, and the author asserts that 'almost every particular circumstance against the then *supposed* offender is most cruelly observed upon and enforced; and had the judge been endeavouring to convict an innocent man of constructive treason, in the persecuting reign of the tyrannical Stuart family, he could not have addressed the jury more unconstitutionally or illegally.'

Strong words, but the writer does not leave it there. He declares that with the spelling out in such a shameless manner of every circumstance against the accused, before the trial had even begun, 'the abilities and integrity of the Grand Jury of the county of Warwick, (were) held in sovereign contempt by our judge... I am of opinion that this judge, by this charge, empoisoned the minds of the Petit, as well as of the Grand Jury ... against the UNTRIED prisoner, as much as the prisoner could then fairly be supposed to have poisoned the body of the deceased.'

Turning to the summing up at the end of the trial itself, the writer is equally unsparing. Quoting the judge's declaration that he owes it to both the public and the jury to state what 'impressions' the evidence has made on him and to favour them with his personal 'observations' on this, the author insists that 'no, notwithstanding the judge speciously informs the jury that they are not to adopt *his* opinion; no, notwithstanding the judge so informs the jury that they are to consider the evidence *themselves*; no, notwithstanding the judge so informs the jury that they are to form their own opinions; no, notwithstanding the judge so informs the jury that if they differ from him in one, in any, or in all the reasons he gives, that it is *their* judgement, and not his, that must decide the cause:

notwithstanding the judge gives the jury all these specious informations, yet the constitution of England holds that judge a contemner of law, who so directs a jury.'

'A Lawyer' cites in particular the judge's comparison of the medical evidence and his adverse comments on that of Mr Hunter. There was no reminder of the contrast in experience and standing between the practitioners who took part in the autopsy and that of 'the ablest anatomist in Europe.' The judge, he says, should have reminded the jury that both Dr Rattray and Mr Wilmer had felt that, given the extreme state of putrefaction, no firm opinion could be formed as to the cause of death. And so, when Buller criticises Mr Hunter's admission of doubt, 'I take leave to say it is a more convincing (though not quite so positive an evidence) than that of the gentlemen of the faculty.'

The author was of course relying on the written records of the trial, and he takes no account of the *impression* that Hunter must inevitably have made on both the judge and jury, who will have been struck by the contrast between the self-assurance with which he ended his evidence-in-chief, declaring unequivocally that the appearance of the corpse, as described by those present at the exhumation, 'does not give the least suspicion' of poison, with his abject admission just a few minutes later, after his mauling under the 'distressing' cross-examination that, 'I can give nothing decisive.'

Nevertheless, 'A Lawyer' is surely right when he accuses the judge of going against one of the most basic tenets of English law, 'that in doubtful cases, and especially in those of blood, the balance ought always to preponderate in favour of the prisoner.'

The writer concludes that, leaving aside suppositions and inferences, on the evidence presented to the court it had not been proved that Sir Theodosius had been murdered at all. But even if this was the case, and Donellan was responsible, 'is it not better that even ninety-nine guilty persons escape, than that the hundredth *innocent* person should be condemned? For the protection of the innocent, and not the punishment of the guilty, is the end of all law.'

For others though Donellan's guilt was irrefutable. Whatever the failings of the judge – and very few voices were raised in his defence – the Crown had made its case, with virtually all the evidence leading to only one possible conclusion. The April 1781 edition of the *Westminster Magazine* which, as usual, promised 'a greater variety of New and Original ESSAYS and CURIOUS PRODUCTIONS than are to be found in any other Periodical Publication whatever', had as its lead article *An Account of Captain John Donnellan* and the opening paragraph makes it abundantly clear which side of the argument it is on:

> 'To the lasting infamy of the present times, we are constrained to record the circumstances of an act scarcely to be paralleled for its wickedness in the annals of the world; of a crime at which human nature shudders with horror, as being perpetrated deliberately in cold blood, upon motives the most base, and in a manner of all others the most shocking.'

The writer gives short shrift to those who were already expressing doubts about the validity of the evidence. After briefly summarising the case against the accused, he declares that, 'These concurring circumstances certainly amount to a legal proof. Should they be deemed insufficient by some lawyers, the most terrible consequences might arise for society. It would be almost permitting with impunity the crime of poisoning; as the actual composition and administration of such infernal doses, must, in many cases, be nearly equal to an impossibility.'

Leaving on one side the circumstantial debate, many commentators were particularly swayed by the medical evidence. Sir Robert Christison, Professor of Medical Jurisprudence at the University of Edinburgh and an expert witness at many murder trials where poison was suspected, was far from impressed by Mr Hunter's testimony. In his *Treatise on Poisons*, published in 1829, he states, 'I must frankly observe that (his) evidence does him very little credit, and his high professional eminence is the very reverse of a reason for palliating his errors or treating them with the lenity which they have received from his numerous critics.'

Later in the century, in 1890, Sir Willoughby Maycock devoted a chapter to the case in his *Celebrated Crimes and Criminals*. He was a civil servant and diplomat and was not concerned with medical or legal niceties, contenting himself with a straightforward account of the affair. He does concede that the judge's summing up was 'dead against' the prisoner but even so has no doubt that the verdict was correct, dismissing Donellan's 'Defence', as read to the jury, as 'a mere rambling one-sided statement of occurrences on which the evidence already adduced threw a very different complexion... A more feeble defence could hardly be conceived. Not a word about the laurel water, not a suggestion as to how Sir Theodosius had died.' Clearly, Maycock had not read Donellan's posthumous '*Defence*', where both of these points are tackled, whether convincingly or not.

But the misgivings refused to go away. Another to express serious doubts was S.M.Phillips, who in 1815 prefaced his *Famous Cases of Circumstantial Evidence* with *An Introduction on the Theory of Presumptive Proof.* The main body of the work considers twenty-seven trials, in both Europe and America and going back over a century, where accused individuals, all of them found guilty on entirely circumstantial evidence, and most of them executed, were later found to be innocent.

In the Introduction, where the general principles of the role of circumstantial evidence are considered, Phillips takes as a prime example 'the celebrated trial of Captain Donellan.'

Like 'A Lawyer' he acknowledges that Donellan might well have committed the crime but even so, in his view, he was the victim of a gross miscarriage of justice. And the blame for this he lays squarely at the door of Mr Justice Buller. The latter's assertion to the jury that 'a presumption, which necessarily arises from circumstances, is very often more convincing, and more satisfactory, than any other kind of evidence' is not only 'new to the practice of English law' but 'repugnant to the received principles of jurisprudence.'

The entire Prosecution case was, he declares, based on assumptions. 'During the whole course of this celebrated trial, there was not a single fact established by evidence, except the death, and the convulsive appearances at the moment.' And Mr Hunter testified that these 'offered no suspicion of poison, and were generally incident to sudden death, in what might be called a state of health; not only there was no fact proved, but there was not one single circumstance proved.'

Facts, asserts Phillips, must take precedence over assumptions. Sir Theodosius 'was supposed to be poisoned, because it was believed to be laurel water; and it was believed to be laurel water, because he was supposed to be poisoned.' But this equation was built on conjecture because there was no factual proof of either of the suppositions, reliant as they were on the evidence of one individual in a state of considerable mental 'distraction', arising from the death of her son. Lady Boughton had momentarily detected an aroma like that of bitter almonds, but 'what so uncertain as the sense of smell? Of all the human senses, it is the most uncertain, the most variable, and fallacious.'

Dr Parsons, expert witness for the Crown, admitted that he based his opinion solely on her description, but 'that modest and eminent man', Mr Hunter, drawing on his vastly superior experience, gave a far more qualified response. He could go no further than to say, 'If I knew that the draught was poison, I should say, most probably, that the symptoms arose from that; but when I don't know that that draught was poison, when I consider that a number of other things might occasion his death, I cannot answer positively to it.'

Phillips contrasts this expression of honest doubt, which so exasperated the judge, with the certainty of the Prosecution's medical witnesses, singling out Dr Rattray for particular opprobrium. 'But, unfortunately, it is a matter of pride, in some men, to be always certain in their opinion, and to appear beyond the influence of doubt.'

In conclusion, he states, 'We have been the more full in our observations on this trial, because it has been so often quoted with a sort of triumph, as forming a model and illustration of the nature of circumstantial evidence. It is an illustration, indeed, of how little evidence one man has been convicted on; but it is an illustration of nothing else. We can never bring ourselves to believe, that it is necessary to forfeit the life of a man on bare suspicion, on presumptions without proof, and on inferences unsupported by evidence.'

Virtually coinciding with Donellan's *Defence*, there appeared, first in April in two of the public prints, the *Westminster* and the *Political* magazines, then shortly afterwards in complete format *The Life of Capt. John Donnellan, late Master of the Ceremonies at the Pantheon, Convicted of the Murder of Sir Theod. Edwd. Allesley Boughton, Bt, at the Assizes held at Warwick, Friday the 30th of March, 1781: including an Account of Capt. Donnellan's Transactions in the East-Indies.*

Nearly all of its ninety-six pages had clearly been written before the trial, with just a hastily added Postscript recording the verdict and reproducing the newspaper accounts of the execution. Whilst the *Defence* had Donellan's posthumous blessing, the author of this 'unauthorised' biography takes a very different line, consistently portraying his subject in the most negative possible light. The *Defence* skates over Donellan's earlier career, first in India, with no reference to his court-martial, then in London, but the *Life* describes these episodes with great relish. Taking his cue from Captain Bobadil, the military braggart in Ben Jonson's comedy *Every Man in his Humour,* the writer dismisses Donellan's own account of his Indian exploits as the mere 'gasconade of a Bobadil'.

Once in London, 'the circle of his friends had lately been much enlarged by his introduction to the gay and polite world…. Dress and gaming engrossed his whole attention, and he soon had an opportunity of placing himself in a very distinguished situation – that of Director of the Entertainments at the Pantheon. In this station, to execute the duties of which no abilities are necessary, and where the less a person is incumbered with learning or genius the better chance he has of acquiring the applause of the world, Captain Donellan presided for some years.' Through his 'extravagant vanity' his financial situation became 'greatly injured' so that 'play and gallantry, the ultimate subterfuges of dissipation, were his general resources' culminating in his unscrupulous resolve to marry an heiress and all that followed.

Much of the *Life* reads like a melodramatic fiction, and the case did in fact catch the attention of two of the nineteenth century's best known novelists. Between 1859 and 1870 Charles Dickens published a weekly journal, *All the Year Round*, then after his death his son, also Charles, took it over. The contents were a mix of fiction – *A Tale of Two Cities* and *Great Expectations*, as well as *The Moonstone* and *The Woman in White* by Wilkie Collins were first serialised here – and factual articles on a variety of themes, with several regular anonymous contributors in addition to Dickens himself. One such feature had the title *The Little Bottle of Laurel Water, a Story of Lawford Hall*.

It is a straightforward retelling of the familiar story, leaning heavily on the trial records and the *Life*. It accepts his guilt without question, portraying him throughout as the villain of the piece. At the Pantheon 'he was in all his glory; smooth, graceful, stealthy as a snake.' Then, to mix the metaphors, after his arrest he 'turned and doubled with the cunning of a wounded hare.' Awaiting his trial, he behaved 'as might have been expected, smoothly, wickedly, and grasping like a lying coward at any means of escape.'

Reaching the night before the execution, the writer – not, one hopes, Dickens himself – indulges in a final flight of fantasy. The two keepers accompanying him in the condemned cell fall asleep, whereupon 'the murderer threw himself upon his knees, and prayed fervently for a considerable time. Who may not say he did not repent? But he made no confession.'

Some twenty years earlier, in 1848, there had appeared a three-volume novel by G.P.R.James, *Sir Theodore Broughton; or Laurel Water*. James was a prolific writer who, in his day, vied for popularity with Dickens but he has now fallen into merciful obscurity. As the title clearly shows, he was trading here on what he himself describes as the 'too-celebrated tragedy of Lawford Hall.'

In a Preface, he tells how he had long been fascinated by the story, but was a third of the way through writing the novel before he read Gurney's record of the trial and this confirmed his doubts about the outcome. Whilst not being at all certain of Donellan's innocence, he was convinced that the Prosecution had not proved their case and the verdict was a clear miscarriage of justice.

However, emulating Wilkie Collins' dictum as regards his readers to 'make 'em wait', this element of a highly convoluted plot does not feature until the very end of the third volume, with the fatal potion itself not putting in an appearance until the penultimate chapter. Before that we have a typical Victorian romance, complete with a swooning, long-lost heiress saved from the jaws of death in a shipwreck by a strong, silent hero, a highwayman in disguise, an attempted kidnapping, the destruction of an inn by fire, and assorted deathbed scenes.

We first meet Sir Theodore at the age of fourteen, when he inherits the baronetcy and a large fortune from his grandfather. As an orphan (there is no Lady Boughton-like character) he is put under the charge of his unmarried cousin, and heir if he should die without issue, Captain Tom Donovan, who is twenty years his senior and had himself expected to inherit the old man's money. The family seat, Ashton Hall, is in Warwickshire but beyond that James is imprecise. Part of the action does take place at Dunchurch and Stratton (Stretton)-on-Dunsmore, both within a million miles of Little Lawford, but James' hold on geography is tenuous, for he places Ludlow between Ashton Hall and London!

Theodore, like his real-life counterpart, is 'a sad scape-grace, and weak, very weak', although his worst crime up to this point seems to have been shooting half a score of his grandfather's fowls with a bow and arrow. Donovan is portrayed in an ambivalent fashion – angry and bitter at being overlooked in the will but trying his best to keep the youth on the straight and narrow. Very reluctantly, for he is en route to France at the time to indulge his own vices, he intervenes to extricate his charge from a duel where he would almost certainly have come off second-best.

This occurs in London, with the story having moved on five years. Donovan has sent his ward there, in the care of his unscrupulous tutor, Dr Gamble, and a villainous manservant, Zachary Hargrave, both of whom have been instructed to introduce the young man to the less salubrious elements of high society. Initially, Theodore's greatest crime is to 'insult' a lady by telling her she is beautiful without their having been formally introduced. But he does fall into a life of dissipation and, egged on by Gamble, he traps the same young woman into consenting to marry him, even though she is in love with our missing-presumed-dead hero.

It is when Donovan learns of this that the novel finally nears its climax. With his usual uneasy mix of motives – genuine disgust at Theodore's behaviour, together with the need to keep him single – he forbids the marriage until the youth comes of age. It is as this approaches that he learns of the value of laurel water as 'the speediest, quietest, most comfortable sort of death in the world ... for it leaves no marks.' He picks cherry-laurel leaves and distils them but then 'a fit of indescribable agitation' seizes him, and he only calms himself with the thought that the concoction need not actually be used.

Theodore meanwhile has continued his degenerate life-style in Warwickshire, and a local doctor has prescribed a potion which he has placed on his dressing-room mantelpiece. He has also berated Hargraves, threatening to dismiss him once he comes of age.

The servant reports this to Donovan, who assures him, in terms reminiscent of Donellan's supposed exchange with the gardener, that, 'If I were master here, you should have a different prospect.' Continuing the parallels, Theodore goes fishing, not returning until it is nearly dark, and Donovan declares to the footman, 'He will kill himself, that is clear. He is greatly changed. His death would not surprise me any day.'

In an agony of doubt, constantly muttering, 'No, no, no,' he takes the still, pours the liquid into a tumbler and fills the still with quicklime, before retiring for the night. Hargrave though is still awake, moving stealthily into the room and taking the tumbler. He feeds a small amount to a cat, which dies instantly, then creeps up to Theodore's dressing-room and substitutes the poison for the medicine.

Early next morning, with Donovan about to go out riding, he is called to the room, where the young man is 'all gasping and heaving, and foaming at the mouth' before, within a few minutes, dying. In the presence of two maidservants, Donovan snatches up the phial, recognises the smell of laurel water and in a blind panic ('Who could have given it to him? Could he himself have done it in his sleep?') takes another bottle from one of the maids, tastes the contents and washes both of them out.

The tragic outcome is related in one brief paragraph:

> 'Captain Donovan, conscious of intended guilt, was betrayed into such doubtful conduct after the death of his ward, that suspicion was soon directed towards himself. He was tried by a judge who summed up harshly against him, convicted upon evidence that would not in our days be held conclusive, and executed for a crime he had meditated, but did not commit, protesting his innocence to the last.'

7. *The Pantheon, Oxford Street façade, by Thomas Girth.*

8. *A masqued entertainment at the Pantheon, devised by Donellan as
Master of the Ceremonies, by Charles White.*

9. *Sir Theodosius Boughton (contemporary print).*

10. *John Donellan (contemporary print).*

11. *Lawford Hall (contemporary print).*

12. *The Avon below the site of Lawford Hall, where Theodosius spent his last evening 'a-fishing'.*

Thos. [illegible] bury June [illegible]

Mr. [illegible] bury June [illegible]

Elizabeth Essex bury'd July 7th
John Crofts bury'd August 5th
Thomas Slater bury'd August 31st
William Lester bury'd Oct. 12th
Theodocia King Donnellan bury'd Oct. 20th
Thomas Lilume? bury'd Dec. 9th

1780
Elizabeth Gibbs bury'd Jan. 3d
Esther Van bury'd Feb. 18th
John Walker bury'd March 15th
Elizabeth Atkins buried March 16th
Solomon Peasey bury'd April 22d
John Main bury'd May 21st
William Crofts bury'd May 30th
Grace Bucknall bury'd June 7th
Elizabeth Burgess bury'd June 8th
Mary Bolton bury'd July 3d
Edward Minors bury'd July 21st
Sr. Theo: Ed: Alle: Boughton bury'd Sep: 6th

1781
Mary Norman bury'd Jan 5th

13. *Extract from the Newbold-on-Avon parish register for 1779-80, recording the burials of Donellan's infant daughter Theodosia and Sir Theodosius.*

14. *The crucial 'bottle rinsing' episode, with Theodosius on his death-bed (contemporary print).*

THE

PROCEEDINGS AT LARGE

ON THE

TRIAL

OF

JOHN DONELLAN, Esq.

FOR THE WILFUL MURDER

(BY POISON) OF

Sir THE. EDWARD ALLESLEY BOUGHTON,
BART.

LATE OF LAWFORD-HALL, IN THE COUNTY OF
WARWICK.

TRIED BEFORE

Mr. JUSTICE BULLER,

AT THE ASSIZES at WARWICK.

ON FRIDAY THE 30th DAY OF MARCH, 1781.

Taken in Short-hand, by Permiſſion of the Judge,
By W. BLANCHARD.

LONDON.

Printed for J. Almon and J. Debrett, oppoſite Burlington
Houſe in Piccadilly, R. Baldwin and J. Bew in Paternoſter-
Row, J. Sewell in Cornhill, and Mr. Blanchard No. 4,
Dean-Street, Fetter Lane; and ſold alſo by Mr. Luckman
at Coventry, and the other Bookſellers in Coventry; Bir-
mingham; Stratford, &c.

PRICE TWO SHILLINGS.

15. *Title page of trial transcript.*

16. *John Donellan (contemporary print).*

A

DEFENCE

AND

Subſtance of the Trial

OF

JOHN DONNELLAN, Eſq;

WHO WAS CONVICTED FOR THE

MURDER

OF

Sir THEODOSIUS BOUGHTON, Bart.

AT THE

ASSIZES held at *WARWICK,*

On FRIDAY the 30th of MARCH 1781,

BEFORE

The Hon. FRANCIS BULLER, Eſq;

One of his Majeſty's Juſtices of the Court of KING's-BENCH.

Founded on the CASE ſolemnly atteſted by the Sufferer after his
Conviction, and publiſhed at the Requeſt of his Solicitors,

Meſſrs. INGE and WEBB.

LONDON:

Printed for JOHN BELL, at the BRITISH LIBRARY, STRAND.
M. DCC. LXXXI.
[PRICE THREE SHILLINGS AND SIXPENCE.]

17. *Title page of Donellan's posthumous* Defence.

Chapter Seventeen

WITHOUT IN any way accepting James's version of events, sheer fiction as he himself acknowledges, his misgivings about the outcome of the trial were surely justified. Despite Donellan's best efforts to incriminate himself, there remained enough of the essential element of reasonable doubt to make the guilty verdict unsound. The prejudicial publicity and unsubstantiated rumours, the bias and ineptitude of the judge, the gross inadequacy of the Defence, and the unconvincing performance of their star witness all conspired to destroy any chance of a fair trial. But however impartial the judge might have been or skilful the Defending Counsel, the fact that the jury reached their verdict in such a scandalously short time shows that Donellan's cause was lost from the outset.

But if he had walked free from the court into Northgate Street, in the shadow of the collegiate church of St Mary, how would he have fared? What would have been the reaction of the mob, assembled outside the courthouse and eagerly awaiting only one acceptable verdict? In his letter of 24th March he speaks of celebrating his release with his London friends, but as his application to Colonel Forde after his court-martial showed, he had a very thick skin and could well have seen no problem in returning to Lawford Hall.

But would he have been welcomed back, to take up where he had so abruptly left off six months earlier, reunited with his wife and children and running the estate, at least until the new baronet took up his inheritance? And what of his relationship with Lady Boughton, whom he had in his extremity indicted as the actual murderer? One wonders how long such a situation could have lasted.

He could well, of course, have been guilty. He had both motive and opportunity, and his previous history does not inspire any great confidence in either his moral standards or veracity. Also, apart from the motives put forward by the Crown, one further point that seems not to have occurred to anyone at the time – or since

– is that he might have been acting on behalf of his son. Even if it is true, as he asserted, that he had given up all claim to his wife's property and inheritance (and no evidence was ever produced to confirm this) it is a fact that his increasingly pessimistic warnings about Theodosius's state of health coincided with baby John's birth. He was clearly a devoted father and a desire to provide as well as possible for his son just might have been the tipping point for his decision to act.

If by any chance though, he was not the killer, who had brought about Sir Theodosius's death? Lady Boughton? Having seen the sufferings of her husband, afflicted by the same venereal complaint, had she in a twisted act of compassion saved her son from a similar fate? Surely not. Foolish woman, weak mother, inadequate witness, yes, but it is impossible to see her as the cold-blooded poisoner of her only son. And what of Theodosia, that shadowy figure who does not utter a single word in any of the contemporary documents? As the sole heir of a considerable fortune she had the greatest motive of anyone, but there is not a scintilla of evidence to link her with the crime. Or there is James's solution – a disgruntled servant. Donellan had hinted at this briefly, but again there is not the slightest indication that any of the servants, male or female, bore the slightest grudge against the young baronet.

There are, however, other possibilities. The Defence, following Donellan's own immediate reaction, tried to argue that Theodosius died from natural causes, that the convulsions and foaming at the mouth were signs of a stroke or an epileptic fit. Mr Hunter supported this, partly on the grounds that the youth's father, albeit some thirty years older, died in this fashion. It will be recalled that Theodosius's grandfather also died young – he was just thirty-two – and that his death could have been precipitated by a venereal disease. The victim had himself suffered from this since his mid-teens – or even earlier if it was inherited – and it is certainly clear that his health was much more precarious than the Prosecution claimed.

This opens up another possibility that Donellan tentatively put forward then discarded – suicide. One of the main side effects of syphilis is mental imbalance, and Theodosius's increasingly erratic behaviour, allied with his carelessness for his own well-being – the duel challenges, the swimming in the reed-infested pond, the church tower episode – strongly suggest that he was affected in this way. Along with the venereal disease, he might have inherited this from his grandfather, whose sanity was the subject of much speculation.

And if Lady Boughton's fears were justified and he really was contemplating marriage to Miss Fonnereau, this could have brought home to him the stark reality of his condition. If Donellan is to be believed, his despair at the state he had been reduced to is vividly shown in an encounter with his mother just two days before his death, when he 'wept bitterly, saying that if he should get the better of his complaints, he would lead quite a new life.'

His apparent cheerfulness on the night prior to his death, and even the next morning, is also typical of the violent mood swings of someone in his mental state, and if he had indeed chosen to take this way out, the new-found resolve could have resulted in a more settled frame of mind. His involvement of his mother in administering the fatal draught and inevitably witnessing his dying agony is more difficult to explain, unless this was a final macabre practical joke played on a person whose ineffectual attempts to reform him he might well, in a contorted way, have come to resent.

Certainly, he had the means, with ready access to at least one form of poison – arsenic. It would be a supreme irony if this, which was identified both at the Inquest and in the Indictment before the trial, was the actual instrument all along. The only reason for abandoning it in favour of laurel water was Lady Boughton's comparison of the smell with bitter almonds, and as she demonstrated with alarming frequency she was not the most infallible of judges.

Yet another possibility is that Theodosius's death was caused by misadventure; that the medical treatments he was receiving inadvertently killed him. His constant 'quacking' of himself with mercurial ointment, which Mr Powell was dismayed to hear about, was in itself potentially lethal. Donellan's gloomy pronouncement to the Revd Newsam that this was the immediate cause of the young man's decline, so that his blood was 'a mass of mercury and corruption', might well have been correct.

And even if it was not in itself life-threatening, there could well have been a fatal reaction when the apothecary's concoctions were added. Lady Boughton's immediate reaction to her son's convulsions was 'that it was an unaccountable thing in the doctor to send such a medicine, for if it had been taken by a dog it would have killed him.' Her suspicions were soon to be focused on Donellan, but her initial fears might in fact have been justified.

Although the medical men accepted without question that the various items Powell prescribed, both in isolation and combined, were harmless, this is far from the case. Many of his remedies have been abandoned by present day practitioners because of the dangers they pose. When he was first called in, he treated his patient with tablets of calomel. This white crystalline powder was considered an effective purgative but its use was fraught with danger for it can readily decompose into the highly toxic mercuric chloride. The side-effects were frequently confused with that of the original syphilis and proved fatal on many occasions.

After several weeks, still attempting to achieve a cleansing effect, Powell added a mixture of jalap (bindweed) and rhubarb. As with the mercury, such a remedy had to be treated with great caution. Rhubarb contains a blend of acids including oxalic, and eating the leaves in particular can have injurious even fatal results. Similarly, the purgative action of bindweed is unpredictable and highly dangerous and herbal practitioners warn nowadays against its use.

It is easy to see why Donellan, with his past history and suspect behaviour at key moments of the crisis precipitated by Theodosius's death, was immediately identified as the culprit. However, any halfway competent Defence Counsel could have put forward some or all of these alternative hypotheses, sowing the seeds of 'reasonable doubt' in the minds of a fair-minded jury. But it was not to be and we are left to contemplate a trial and verdict that were a gross travesty of justice. And over and above this, the nagging thought remains that Donellan should not simply have been found 'Not Guilty' on a legal technicality but that he was speaking nothing but the truth in his insistent but ultimately unavailing protestations of his innocence.

Epilogue

THE FORTUNES of the other principal players in the drama varied considerably. Despite the widespread criticism of his conduct of the trial – a view reinforced three years later when a retrial was ordered in the case of a charge of seditious libel against the Dean of St Asaph on the grounds that he had misdirected the jury – Francis Buller's career prospered. He was a leading figure on King's Bench, and had the dubious distinction of passing the first sentences of transportation to the newly established penal colony of New South Wales. He was a protégé of Lord Mansfield, the Lord Chancellor, and was widely expected to be his successor. He was disappointed in this but in 1790, as some form of consolation he was made baronet and transferred to the Court of Common Pleas, where he remained until his death in 1800.

In his later years his attention turned to his native Devon. With his wife's money he purchased Prince Hall, a farmhouse near Princetown on Dartmoor, and transformed it into a much grander dwelling befitting the seat of a country gentleman. (It is now a luxury hotel.) He also built an inn on the Packhorse Road between Princetown and Exeter, first named the Saracen's Head, after the crest of the family's coat of arms, and now the Two Bridges Hotel. Prince Hall was surrounded by six hundred inhospitable acres, fit only for sheep and cattle, but by experimenting with the rotation method he attempted to grow a variety of crops, much to the bemusement of the locals. He did succeed in producing turnips of a respectable size, but unfortunately most of them were hollow!

Buller found himself embroiled in fresh controversy when a group of his employees removed from nearby Crockern Tor the huge granite slab which for centuries had formed the table of the Dartmoor tin-miners' Stannary Parliament, together with other rocks that had been used as seats. They were dragged across the moor by a team of oxen, broken up and added to the building work he had commissioned.

The two other leading lawyers at the trial fared less well. Unsurprisingly perhaps, Mr Newnham never achieved any great eminence, while Henry Howarth's much more promising career was cut short just three years later when he drowned in a boating accident in the Thames, near Mortlake, leaving a grieving mistress, Miss Chippendale, daughter of the great cabinet-maker.

Despite his unfortunate courtroom performance, Mr Hunter's reputation remained largely unimpaired. As well as his royal appointment, he became Surgeon-General to the British Army and when he died he was honoured with a funeral in Westminster Abbey, whilst statues were erected in his memory at the University of Oxford and near his former home in Leicester Square.

None of the local medical men rose beyond the level of 'country practitioners', not even Samuel Bucknill, who never achieved the wider recognition he craved. His grandson, Sir John Charles Bucknill, however, became a national figure with a practice in Wimpole Street and a reputation as the leading alienist (a pioneer of psychiatry) of his time. He specialised in mental disorder and, in a curious quirk of fate, played a part in a murder trial that was to grip the public imagination some eighty years after the Donellan case.

Sixteen-year old Constance Kent had pleaded guilty to the horrific murder of her infant step-brother and Bucknill was commissioned by the Defence to examine her in prison to see whether there were grounds for an appeal. In the course of a lengthy interview she made a full confession – the subject of considerable speculation since – but although he concluded that she had inherited from her mother 'a strong tendency to insanity', he complied with her own wishes and advised that there should be no reliance on a plea of this nature. (The death sentence was nonetheless commuted to life imprisonment and after serving twenty-five years she was freed and moved to Australia where she remained until her death.)

In a further twist, venereal disease could have been a crucial factor in both the Donellan and Kent cases. As we have seen, Theodosius's illness could have been congenital, and the inherited insanity that Bucknill noted regarding Constance might well have been the result of the girl's father infecting his first wife, who died insane, aged forty-four, with syphilis. It is possible that he also passed the disease to his second wife, who became paralysed and almost blind before her death at the age of forty-six.

As for the Boughton family, Lady Boughton moved to Bath, where she lived until 1787 and was reunited with her husband and son in the crypt of Newbold church. Theodosia also tried to distance herself from the scandal – metaphorically, at least. She dropped her married name, reverting to the Beauchamp of her mother's family, and also adopted this device for her two surviving children.

Nothing is known of Maria but it seems that she remained unmarried before her early death. The infant John fared slightly better: he went to Oxford, where, as was customary at that time, he took holy orders. He was given responsibility for the estates of Adston and Potterspury, the two Northamptonshire properties that Lady Boughton had brought into the family, but he too died unmarried at the age of twenty-five – yet another male member of the Boughton clan to die young.

Theodosia herself finally emerges from the shadows. With her brother's death, she was an extremely wealthy young woman – still just twenty-three – and was soon for the second time the target of fortune hunters. In 1787 she married an impoverished baronet, Sir Egerton Leigh, whose father had lost most of his possessions in South Carolina in the aftermath of the American War of Independence. They lived at Brownsover Hall, very near Little Lawford, and she readily took on the role of lady of the manor performing numerous good works in the district, whilst supporting her husband, who was a prominent non-conformist. In 1803, for example, she laid the foundation stone of the first Baptist church in Rugby, which he had largely financed. They had two children, a son Egerton who died aged thirteen and a daughter, Theodosia de Malsburgh, named after Sir Egerton's younger sister, who had married Baron von Malsburgh of Hesse Cassel.

After his death in 1818, she divided her time between Warwickshire and her town house in Montague Square. In middle age she developed a fixation for Napoleon Buonaparte. He died on St Helena in 1821 but, presumably in order to bring him within touching distance, she married Barry O'Meara, the surgeon who had attended him in exile. He came to her attention in 1822 with the publication of his book *Napoleon in Exile*, in which he strongly criticised the treatment the former Emperor had received under the governorship of Sir Hudson Lowe. He was threatened with a libel suit but this did not materialise, and in any case financial matters would not have concerned him unduly for he married Theodosia the following year.

O'Meara was, of course, her second Irish-born husband, and once again there was a wide age discrepancy although in the second case it was she who was the older, by some thirty years! Her choice of marriage partners gave rise to much would-be humorous comment, with the three known as the Pendent, the Independent and the Dependent.

She died in January 1830 and was buried at Newbold. The entry in the parish register names her as 'Dame Theodosia Beauchamp Leigh, wife of Barry O'Meara, Esqre, Brownsover and Montague Square, London', and a plaque in Newbold church, honouring her second husband, also commemorates 'Dame Theodosia Beauchamp, wife of the first-named Sir Egerton Leigh, Bart.'

In neither instance is there any reference to her first marriage, and just as attempts have been made to expunge Donellan from his father's family records, so he has been virtually deleted from the annals of the Boughton dynasty. There is just one fleeting reference in an abstract of Theodosia's title to her brother's estates, and in the family history *Memorials of a Warwickshire Family* by Bridgeman Boughton-Leigh, published in 1906, we simply learn that Sir Theodosius 'went to Rugby School, and afterwards to Eton, and died unmarried shortly before gaining his majority.' The nature of his death is relegated to a reluctant footnote, where we are told that 'he was poisoned in the year 1780, at Lawford Hall, with laurel-water essence, and buried at Newbold-on-Avon about a fortnight afterwards.' But there is no clue that the alleged perpetrator was none other than the husband of 'Dame Theodosia Beauchamp.'

Theodosius's successor Sir Edward, the eighth baronet, chose to remain in Herefordshire and Lawford Hall was sold to John Caldecott of Rugby, the family's solicitor and the very man who had instructed the Prosecution in Donellan's trial. But he in turn did not live there. Gossip was already adding a second ghost to keep company with One-Handed Boughton, and in 1784 the house, considered by locals to be a place a-cursed, was razed to the ground

All that remain are a few humps and bumps in a field running down to the river where Theodosius fished that final evening. Some of the ornamental bricks from the Hall were used to construct the waterfall two miles upstream, just below Newbold church, and the stable block has been converted into a house, Little Lawford Hall. It was as he rode on that fateful morning into the former stable yard, which still survives, that Donellan learned of the calamity that had overtaken the family. And was to change his own life for ever.

Notes

PROLOGUE: The description of the exhumation is based on testimony at Donellan's trial, accounts in the public prints, including the *Coventry Mercury*, and Donellan's posthumously published *Defence* (1781).

CHAPTER ONE: Information on the Donellan family is to be found in the O'Connor Donellan Estate Papers. Donellan's *Case*, presented to the Directors of the East India Company in 1770, contains his version of his exploits in India and the defence he mounted at his court-martial. The contrary view is put forward in *The Life of Capt. John Donellan* (1781), which includes in the British Library copy a full account of the court-martial. Contemporary accounts of the siege of Mazulipatam are included in Orme's *History of the British Nation in Indostan, vol.ii*, and *Cambridge's Account of the War in India* (1761).

CHAPTER TWO: The Habeas Corpus writ for the release of Nehemiah Donellan is contained in the records of King's Bench (KB1) in the National Archives, Kew. The correspondence between Donellan and Clive is included in his *Case*. The description of the Pantheon is drawn from the *Survey of London, volumes 31 and 32*. An eye-witness account of Donellan's execution states that he was just 5 feet 4 inches tall, but this was the average height for a man in eighteenth-century England.

CHAPTER THREE: Details of the Boughton family are taken from the parish records of Newbold-on-Avon and Harborough Magna, together with the papers of the Boughton-Leigh family, all of which are located in the Warwickshire County Records Office. Donellan's oldest child, Maria, has proved impossible to trace through the parish records, both in Warwickshire and beyond. However, her absence from the former suggests that she was born before her parents' arrival at Lawford Hall. Sir William Wheler: the contemporary documents relating to the case spell the surname with the more usual double e (taking their cue perhaps from the shorthand accounts of the trial, where other names are misspelt) but the Leamington Hastings parish records and the family papers consistently use a single e so I have followed this form throughout.

The *Life* favours the Pantheon version for Donellan's first meeting with Theodosia. The Bath setting is described in the June 1922 edition of the *Juridical Review*. Donellan's account of his early dealings with the family is given in some detail in his *Defence*.

CHAPTER FOUR: Lady Boughton's version of the events on the evening before Theodosius' death was given in evidence at the trial; Donellan's account is contained in his *Defence*.

CHAPTER FIVE: Full accounts (albeit conflicting) of the death of Theodosius were given at the inquest and trial and also by Donellan in his *Defence*. Newnham Wells: a semi-circular depression in the ground is all that remains of the site today – although a room in a nearby house is reputed to have a particularly fine mosaic floor.

CHAPTER SIX: Details of the abandoned autopsies together with the correspondence between Donellan and Sir William Wheler are taken from testimony given at the trial.

CHAPTER SEVEN: Donellan's *Defence* includes a full account of the inquest, including a record of all the evidence given at the two sessions.

CHAPTER EIGHT: The correspondence in the *Coventry Mercury* is contained in *Letters and Paragraphs printed in the "Coventry Mercury" …relating to Captain John Donellan*, twelve copies of which were 'privately printed' in Leamington in 1845. The Sukey Sparrow episode is narrated in Donellan's *Defence*.

CHAPTER NINE: Information on the Buller and Yarde families is taken from the parish records and papers held in the Devon County Records Office, Exeter. Buller's reputation: in the BBC TV series *Garrow's Law – Tales from the Old*

Bailey (2009 and 2010) chronicling the real-life career of William Garrow, the late-eighteenth-century barrister who pioneered courtroom advocacy on behalf of the accused, the hard-line bigot that he crosses swords with is – Judge Buller.

CHAPTERS TEN – FOURTEEN: The description of the trial is based on the shorthand records of Blanchard and Gurney. There are minor variations, with both paraphrasing some of the evidence, and I have drawn on both versions to give as accurate an account as possible. Eyewitness descriptions of Donellan's execution (all virtually identical) were published in many contemporary prints and journals, including the *Coventry Mercury* and the *Westminster Magazine*. His pre-trial letter and that written to Theodosia from the condemned cell are both reproduced in *The Life*. John Hunter was featured in the Channel 4 series *Genius of Britain* (2010) along with such figures as Isaac Newton and Captain James Cook.

CHAPTERS FIFTEEN – SIXTEEN: Copies of all the works cited are in the British Library's collection and many are also held in the Local Studies sections of Warwickshire and Coventry libraries.

EPILOGUE: The Constance Kent case has been the subject of several full-length studies, including *Saint With Red Hands?* (1954) by Yseult Bridges and Kate Summerscale's *The Suspicions of Mr Whicher* (2008). Buller's activities on Dartmoor are recounted in *Magna Britannia, volume 6*, (1822), Lidford Parish, and William Crossing's *Guide to Dartmoor* (1912 edn).

Bibliography

Contemporary Documents:

Blanchard, W., *The Proceedings at Large on the Trial of John Donellan, Esq....Taken in Short-hand, by permission of the Judge* (London, 1781)

Donnellan, J., *The Case of John Donnellan, Captain of Foot, in the Service of the United Company of Merchants Trading to the East Indies, Humbly Addressed to the Honourable the Court of Directors of the said Company* (London, 1770)

Donellan, J., *A Defence and Substance of the Trial of John Donellan, Esq. who was convicted for the murder of Sir Theodosius Boughton, Bart. at the Assizes held at Warwick on Friday the 30th of March 1781* (London, 1781)

Gurney, J., *The Trial of John Donellan, Esq. For the Wilful Murder of Sir Theodosius Edward Allesley Boughton, Bart.... Taken in Short-hand by Joseph Gurney* (London, 1781)

Anon., *The Life of Capt. John Donnellan, late Master of the Ceremonies at the Pantheon, convicted of the Murder of Sir Theod. Edwd. Allesley Boughton, Bt. at the Assizes held at Warwick, Friday the 30th of March, 1781* (London, 1781)

Public Prints and Journals:

All the Year Round; The Little Bottle of Laurel-Water, a story of Lawford Hall (London, 1873)

Juridical Review (Vol. xxiv, no 2, June 1922) Laurel Water by W. Roughead (Edinburgh, 1922)

Letters and Paragraphs printed in the "Coventry Mercury", in the years 1780 and 1781 relating to Captain John Donellan, convicted of the murder of Sir Theodosius Edward Allesley Boughton, Bart. (Leamington, 1845)

Lloyds Evening Post (London, March/April 1781)

Political Review (London, April 1781)

Westminster Magazine: An Account of Captain John Donnellan (embellished with an elegant engraving) (London, April 1781)

Accounts and Commentaries:

A Lawyer, *The Case of John Donellan, Esquire, impartially considered* (London, 1781)

Christoson, R., *Treatise on Poisons* (London, 1829)

Maycock, Sir Willoughby, *Celebrated Crimes and Criminals* (London, 1890)

Phillips, S.M., *Famous Cases of Circumstantial Evidence: with an introduction on the theory of Presumptive Proof* (London, 1873)

Preedy, G., *The Poisoners or The Death of Sir Thomas Overbury to which is added The Murder of Sir Theodosius Boughton* (London, 1936)

Radzinowicz, L., *A History of Criminal Law and its Administration from 1750* (London, 1948-86 – 5 volumes)

Smith, B., *Warwickshire Murders* (Newbury, 1991)

Thompson, E., *John Donellan 1736-1781*; Rugby Local History Research Group Monograph Series: Number 1 (Rugby, 1993)

Townsend, W.C., The *Lives of Twelve Eminent Judges of the last and present centuries (vol. 1)*, (London, 1816)

Ward-Boughton-Leigh, G.F.C., M*emorials of a Warwickshire Family* (London, 1906)

Fiction:

James, G.P.R., *Sir Theodore Broughton or Laurel Water* (3 vols.), (London, 1848)

Index